D1072094

Socialists and European Integration

LIBRARY OF POLITICAL STUDIES

GENERAL EDITOR: H. VICTOR WISEMAN
Professor of Political Science
University of Exeter

Socialists and European Integration

A study of the French Socialist Party

by Byron Criddle

Assistant Lecturer in Politics,
Aberdeen University

LONDON

ROUTLEDGE AND KEGAN PAUL

NEW YORK: HUMANITIES PRESS

First published 1969
by Routledge & Kegan Paul Ltd
Broadway House, 68-74 Carter Lane
London E.C.4
Printed in Great Britain
by Northumberland Press Limited,
Gateshead

SBN 7100 6423 3 (C)

Contents

Abbreviations *page* vii

Author's note viii

Introduction ix

I Socialism and Europeanism   1
   L'Idée européenne   1
   Socialism   3
   Internationalism   5
   Orthodoxy and revisionism   6

2 The S.F.I.O.'s inheritance   9
   Ideological inheritance   9
   National inheritance   13
   The socialist dilemma and post-war prospects   15

3 The S.F.I.O. and Internationalism   19
   The post-war mood   19
   Blumian internationalism   21
   The theory of the big market   25
   Socialists and the United States of Europe   27

4 Third Force or Western defence   31
   The Marshall Plan—origins of economic
    integration   31
   Third forcism   33
   The Council of Europe   38
   The Atlantic Pact—the rejection of neutralism   41

5 The Europe of the Six   46
   The Schuman Plan   46
   Anti-minimalism   49
   Anti-clericalism   52

v

CONTENTS

6	German Rearmament	56
	The European Defence Community	56
	Traditionalist fears	58
	The cédiste *case*	61
	Party split	67
	Defeat for the leadership	71
	Reappraisal	74

7	From Rélance Européenne to L'Europe des Patries	78
	The Mollet government	78
	The Treaties of Rome	81
	Doctrinal introspection	84
	Gaullism	86

8	Conclusion	91
	The role of socialist ideology	92
	Anti-Communism	95
	Anti-Germanism	98
	Escapist illusion	101

	Chronological summary of European organizations	105
	Suggestions for further reading	109
	Bibliography	111

Abbreviations

Organizations, institutions and parties

C.G.T.	Confédération générale du travail
E.C.E.	Economic Commission for Europe
E.E.C.	European Economic Community
E.C.S.C	European Coal and Steel Community
E.D.C.	European Defence Community
M.R.P.	Mouvement républicain populaire
NATO	North Atlantic Treaty Organization
O.E.E.C.	Organization for European Economic Co-operation
P.C.F.	Parti communiste français
R.P.F.	Rassemblement du peuple français
S.F.I.O.	Section française de l'Internationale ouvrière
U.D.S.R.	Union démocratique et socialiste de la Résistance
W.E.U.	Western European Union

Periodicals, publications and newspapers

B.I.	*Bulletin Intérieur du parti socialiste S.F.I.O.*
Fr.Ob.	*France Observateur*
J.O.	*Journal Officiel de l'Assemblée nationale*
Le Pop.	*Le Populaire*
S.I.I.	*Socialist International Information*

Author's note

This study is written primarily with students of European integration in mind, and therefore assumes a knowledge of the outline history of that process since the war. For those unfamiliar with this, however, a chronology and brief summary of each of the important organizations are included as an appendix, along with a glossary of abbreviations.

Introduction

The purpose of this study is to examine the nature and development of the French Socialist Party's policy towards the measures progressively taken in western Europe since the end of the war to integrate into new 'European' institutions the political, economic and military functions of separate nation-state governments.

To define the policy of a political party can be a somewhat elusive task. Most parties in democratic systems show a natural propensity towards pragmatism in matters of policy, and there is a strong tendency to leave policy decisions and statements to the national spokesmen of the party. Because of these tendencies a party's consistent policy is often difficult to define. For this reason the word 'policy' is treated in its widest sense: conference debates at the national congresses of the party, important in the light of the great emphasis placed on party democracy in the party, debates in the national council and decisions taken by the executive committee, together with speeches made by party leaders, and books or articles written by them in journals and newspapers, comprise in this sense the party's policy.

The essential structure of the study is dictated by its purpose. Firstly, the compatibility of socialism and 'Europeanism' is considered and a necessary distinction made between orthodox Marxist and revisionist socialism. Secondly, the French Socialist Party (Section française de l'Internationale ouvrière) is analysed in terms of the orthodox-revisionist dichotomy, and consideration given to the national political environment in which the party has had to operate. Thirdly, examination is made of the S.F.I.O.'s internationalist theory and of its advocacy of European integration and conclusions drawn as to the consistency of its policy with its internationalist theory and with the rest of its ideology. Further, the political motivations of the majority element of the party which has consistently supported European integration, and of the vociferous minority which has at times opposed it, are examined, and related to the way in which the party had become progressively 'Radicalized' over the years; and finally conclusions are drawn on the implication of the party's European policy for the overall position within the socialist ideological spectrum of a party which has traditionally been regarded as one of the major European socialist parties most hostile to social democratic revisionism, and most loyal to 'orthodox' socialism.

General editor's introduction

This series of monographs is designed primarily to meet the needs of students of government, politics, or political science in Universities and other institutions providing courses leading to degrees. Each volume aims to provide a brief general introduction indicating the significance of its topic, e.g., executives, parties, pressure groups, etc., and then a longer 'case study' relevant to the general topic. First-year students will thus be introduced to the kind of detailed work on which all generalizations must be based, while more mature students will have an opportunity to become acquainted with recent original research in a variety of fields. The series will eventually provide a comprehensive coverage of most aspects of political science in a more interesting and fundamental manner than in the large volume which often fails to compensate by breadth what it inevitably lacks in depth.

This study of the French Socialist Party and European integration is of considerable interest in itself. The author's approach is indicated clearly in his Introduction and needs no elaboration here. The problem of the European Community, however, continues to be of great concern in the U.K., not least to the Labour Party. Is there any parallel between the French acceptance of 'social democratic revisionism' and the increasing pragmatism of the British Labour Party? Is the basis of disagreement the same within each of the two parties? What would be the implications for British socialism of entry to the Common Market? Mr. Criddle does not seek to answer these questions but his book may help others to do so. It is, of course, a first rate study in its own right and as such should be very welcome.

H.V.W.

Sources

Socialist Party
National Congress Reports, 1944-61 (annually), 1961-65 (biennially).
Bulletin Intérieur du parti socialiste S.F.I.O. (Monthly).
Le Populaire: the party's daily newspaper.
La Revue Socialiste: a monthly journal.

Other
France Observateur: a left-wing weekly journal.
Socialist International Information: organ of the Socialist International.
Journel Officiel: daily record of parliamentary debates.

Acknowledgments

The author wishes to acknowledge his debt to all the works mentioned in the bibliography, and particularly to P. M. Williams' and B. D. Graham's scholarly works on French politics.

In addition a debt is acknowledged to the staff at the French Socialist Party's Paris offices for affording access to party records; to M. F. G. Marx of the Institut Français in London; to Mr. Albert Carthy, Secretary-General of the Socialist International; and to members of the Department of Politics at Leicester University where the author originally undertook the research upon which this study is based.

1

Socialism and Europeanism

L'idée européenne

L'idée européenne is a concept which was articulated by
intellectuals centuries before the late 1940's, when the
actions of European politicians gave form to the 'idea'.
The Europe that writers envisaged was not one Europe
but many; there was no agreement of form. Men as different as Burke, Hugo and Grotius had been spokesmen for
the 'idea', yet despite the somewhat heterogeneous nature
of this group of advocates, most of their work revealed at
least three common themes: nostalgia for a united
Christendom; the desire for European peace; and cultural
cosmopolitanism and romanticism. The European idea has
been inspired by concepts such as these, and not merely
by what Hallstein has described as 'the pressure of tech-
nology, increasing interdependence, (and) a growing sense
that in a world of giants, nations on the old scale must
bind together' (Hallstein, 1962, p. 5). These latter, though
clearly important in inspiring the European movement
after the Second World War, do not provide a basis for
understanding the essence of the 'idea', as distinct from
the motivations behind the actions of the modern European politicians.

The earliest spokesmen for the 'idea' were post-Renais-

I

sance thinkers who, in the face of the nationalistic and secular forces unleashed by the Renaissance and Reformation, demonstrated a certain nostalgia for the idea of a united Christendom. For some it was the memory of Charlemagne's *rex pater Europa*, under whom *Europa* and *ecclesia* became closely identified. Pierre Dubois in the early fourteenth century proposed a European confederation ruled by a European Council of 'wise expert and faithful men', representing the 'most Christian Republic'. Sully, in his plan for a *république très chrétienne*, a vast *Europe des patries*, and Leibnitz, who saw the union of Europe as a means of restoring catholicism in the Protestant countries, were further exponents of this hankering after a revival of a united Christendom, and nineteenth-century romantics like Novalis and Chateaubriand re-echoed this theme, the latter calling for a 'European tribunal which would judge nations and monarchs in the name of God'.

The second most common form in which the 'idea' had found expression was the quest for peace. Common to the writings of Dubois, Crucé, Grotius, Sully, Penn and Abbé de St. Pierre, was the idea of a *paix perpétuelle en Europe*, based on an alliance between European sovereigns represented by permanent ambassadors at a European assembly, a European army, and majority voting among the Heads of State (Abbé de St. Pierre). Bentham and Kant also saw united Europe as the bearer of perpetual peace.

The third significant motif, that of cultural cosmopolitanism, was a product of the Age of Reason. Here, the Europe was a Europe increasingly aware of what united it culturally, in the political as well as the purely aesthetic sense. Politically, it was the Europe of the *ancien régime*, of powerful dynastic monarchs ruling over largely agrarian systems, and although this age was that which saw the progressive denudation of autocratic power, even the

2

liberal reactions against the old order were homogeneous, under the intellectual dominance of the Encyclopaedists and other French rationalists. Cultural cosmopolitanism, contributed to by such a phenomenon as the Grand Tour, was reflected in Voltaire's comment that a Frenchman, an Englishman, and a German might be mistaken for inhabitants of the same town, and in Burke's remark that 'no citizen of Europe could altogether be an exile in any part of it'. Europe, to intellectuals such as these, was much more than a geographical expression (see Mayne 1964).

These different motifs of expression have been cited here to demonstrate their diversity, and at the same time to provide the basis for a comparison with socialist thought, that is, to enable a consideration of the compatability of socialism and Europeanism.

Socialism

Socialism, it can be said, is concerned with popular sovereignty. Within this concept cohere the many contingent characteristics of liberty, equality, optimism, rationalism, social compassion, etc. Popular sovereignty in the early nineteenth century was about *political* rights: the Jacobins, the Corresponding Societies, the Chartists and the Mazzinians represented this *political* left. By the mid-nineteenth century, socialists had added to this political left an *economic* left (Blanqui, Marx, Proudhon, etc.). The realization had dawned that a transformation of political institutions alone, without changes in the economic structure, would not effectively establish popular sovereignty (see Caute, 1966, Chapter 2). In the words of G. D. H. Cole, 'the wage-system makes active citizenship impossible for the majority', and of Jean Jaurès, 'Just as all citizens exercise political power in a democratic manner in common, so they must exercise economic power

3

in common as well'. Belief in the primacy of economic popular sovereignty is the distinguishing characteristic of socialism, and this being so, it is difficult to see where socialist thought makes much contact with the themes employed by the 'Europeans', who in the main, have not been concerned with this concept. For example, the vision of Europe as a new Carolingian empire (*viz* Napoleon: 'I have not succeeded to the throne of Louis XIV, but to that of Charlemagne'), or as a united Christendom (*viz* the Holy Alliance of 1815, by the terms of which the three participating powers undertook to consider themselves as members of one Christian nation), had little affinity with the concept of economic popular sovereignty. Napoleon, for instance, although he derived his sovereignty from the people and not from divine right, and subscribed to the ideas of the Rights of Man, was manifestly an élitist and had no concern for economic, as distinct from political, popular sovereignty.

Yet the nineteenth century did produce apparent points of contact between socialists and 'Europeans'. For example, Hugo's plea for the abolition of national frontiers ('the Rhine for all!'), and his call for a United States of Europe, was echoed by socialists who saw war as the product of a system of competing nation states. But few political ideologies have advocated war. The French socialist, Proudhon, went some way in synthesizing socialism and federalism in his book *Du Principe fédératif* (1863), where he attacked nationalism and expounded federalism as the 'supreme guarantor of all liberty and of all law', stating that it should 'without soldiers or priests, replace both feudal and Christian society'. Proudhon, however, exponent of an obtuse form of mutualist anarchism, was hardly representative of much socialist thinking in the mid-nineteenth century.

Internationalism

If no points of convergence between socialism and Europeanism have yet been identified, a link may well be found in internationalism. Socialism is allegedly internationalist; Europe is an expression of internationalism; in the nineteenth century therefore, the forces of internationalism were free to join the quest for European unity. This thesis is vulnerable to attack on two counts: firstly, the record of socialists on internationalism is one of extreme ambiguity and ambivalence; and secondly, wherever the commitment to internationalism was expressed in action, it had, as in the case of *Société Démocratique Française* in 1848, the aim of liberating Europe by a revolutionary war of conquest, and the creation of a Europe starkly different from that of the romantics, idealists and federalists. Furthermore, 'workers of all countries, unite!' did not appear necessarily to mean even unity. Marx, despite his dictum that 'the working classes have no country', himself held that 'the chimeras of a European republic, of perpetual peace under a political organization, have become as grotesque as talk of the union of peoples under the aegis of universal free trade'. In fact, the history of socialist parties all over Europe is replete with instances of divergence from the internationalist ideal. In 1870 Engels supported the Germans against the French; in 1918 the S.P.D. deputies ratified the imperialistic Treaty of Brest Litovsk imposed on a Russia which was far from under Tsarist domination. In 1936, when obliged to face the challenge of internationalism posed by the Spanish Civil War, Léon Blum declared 'my soul is torn' and kept his Popular Front government out of the struggle.

Orthodoxy and revisionism

Faithlessness to theory apart, the confusion of socialists over internationalism reflected the division of the socialist movement. Internationalism developed different meanings for different socialists, with the division of the Left into its revolutionary and evolutionary wings, which had parted on the issue of the truth or falsity, the relevance or irrelevance, of dialectical materialism. To the orthodox Marxist, socialism implied a revolutionary struggle to emancipate the proletariat from its economic, and therefore, its political, social and cultural bondage. It implied a total refashioning of society. To the evolutionary, Bernsteinian or Jaurèsian socialist, who rejected the primacy of the economic factor, who progressively shed any belief in revolution, and who by accepting the structure of liberal democratic institutions came increasingly to defend those institutions, it meant the pursuit of the 'bourgeois' values of the French Revolution, of liberty, equality and fraternity; in fact the pursuit of essentially political goals. Committed involvement and action in the liberal democratic parliamentary system, concerned as that system was with the attainment of immediate political objectives, altered the applicability of socialist ideology. Revisionists, proclaiming the ideals of 1789, whilst realizing that the attainment of them required changes in the economic as well as the political structure, tended by their disbelief in the necessary primacy of the economic factor to become preoccupied with gradualism. Thus they tended to neglect the pressing of economic demands, and to concentrate on the fulfilment of the desire for political liberties and universal suffrage, and the full participation of socialists in the political system.

Revisionism however made more than the negative impact the term implies. To the 'economic' factor of Marx-

6

ism, it added the 'moral' factor. In Jaurès' words, 'I do not grant to Marx that religious, political and moral conceptions are solely the reflection of economic phenomena: there is within man such an interpenetration of the man himself and his economic milieu that one cannot separate the economic from the moral life. You can no more dissociate humanity's ideal life from its economic life than you can cut a man in two and thereby dissociate his organic life from the life of his consciousness.' It was this strong idealistic, moral element of the revisionist case which fashioned internationalism in a revisionist mould. Internationalism was not, as it was for the orthodox Marxists, the projection of a mechanistically-determined, economic phenomenon on to a world stage; it was not the fraternity of wage-labourers *qua* wage-labourers. Rather, was it a conception based upon the idealistic and utopian belief in the nobility of man's reason and the perfectibility of human nature. It was humanitarian universalism as opposed to proletarian solidarity; in essence it was a theme of the political, rather than the economic, Left, and was closer in spirit to the doctrine of the Rights of Man than to the Communist Manifesto.

The hypothesis, then, is that its preoccupation with essentially political goals, a preoccupation reflected in its internationalist policies, has made revisionist socialism much less incompatible with 'Europeanism' than orthodox Marxism, which is essentially in pursuit of economic goals incompatible with any forms in which the 'European idea' has been expressed. Furthermore, the pragmatic and gradualist spirit of revisionist socialism has made its exponents more ready to accept temporary limitations in the attainment of its ends. Thus it is that the concept of 'Europe' is acceptable as a stage towards a universal order, whereas to the Marxist parties 'Europe' is an illogical construction irreconcilable with Marxist theory. This hypo-

7

thesis does appear to have been vindicated, in that it has been the revisionist socialist parties which have become active in the European venture since the war. The specific role of their internationalist instincts is of course difficult to define. Pro-Europeanism could be as much an expression of extensive, wholesale doctrinal revision, as of the belief in the universalist concept. Some parties, for example the French, have produced theorists, like Jaurès and Blum, who have fashioned from the old revolutionary internationalism the new humanitarian philosophy, which may have contributed in part to the S.F.I.O.'s acceptance and advocacy of European integration, but it remains the case that Europeanism and unrevised socialism have not been of basically similar inspiration: the one élitist, the other populist; the one appealing to cultural and romantic, the other to rational and material forces; the one inspired by religion, the other by secularism; the one concerned with politics, the other with economics.

2

The S.F.I.O.'s inheritance

In the tension between its 'orthodox' and 'revisionist' wings the French Socialist Party (S.F.I.O.) represents better than any other of the European socialist parties, save possibly the Belgian, the essential socialist dilemma. It possesses an excessively divided inheritance in which the reformist and humanitarian idealism of Jaurès is allied to the doctrinaire theoreticism of Guesde, and where the pluralist and syndicalist views of Proudhon exist alongside the scientific socialism of Marx (Pickles, 1960, p. 74). In addition, the party not only has this divided *ideological* inheritance, but an exceedingly divided *national* inheritance as well, in that it shares, with some other French parties, the problem of operating coherently within a political system as divided over fundamentals as the French political system traditionally has been.

Ideological inheritance

Although it is not possible to be as dogmatic in describing the S.F.I.O. as 'revisionist' (or 'reformist') as it is in so categorizing the German S.P.D., or the British Labour and the Scandinavian social democratic parties, it is certainly true that the party has long ceased to be revolutionary in all but words, and that if its goals have in theory remained revolutionary, its tactics have been undeniably, and without obvious exception, reformist. Of all the European socialist parties the S.F.I.O. has been the most verbally resistant to the reformist cause, and has yet, by its actions, belied its words.

The party was formed in 1905 as a fusion of Guesdist (revolutionary and Marxist) and Jaurèsian (possibilist, participationist and republican) factions. The attempt to form a united socialist party had been in progress for almost two decades, but so deep had been the cleavage over ideology, and therefore tactics, that the achievement of unity had been elusive. The cleavage in the ranks of French socialism in the last decade of the nineteenth century was symbolized and highlighted in two particular issues: the Dreyfus case and the Millerand affair. In the Dreyfus case the 'Dreyfusards' represented to Jaurès a decisive struggle of the progressive forces against military and clerical reaction, of democrats against autocrats, republicans against anti-republicans. To Guesde, the affair was but a conflict between rival bourgeois factions—opportunists (Jewish capitalists) against clericals (anti-semites)—both of whom were enemies of the working class. To Jaurès, the affair was an occasion for socialists to rally with radicals to the defence of the Republic and to stand up and declare faith in human rights (Jaurès, 1906, p. 168); to Guesde the whole affair was a bourgeois red-herring. It is significant that in the Dreyfus affair the Jaurèsian faction won the day, and that in the considerable influx of young aesthetes and intellectuals who joined the party via the Dreyfusards, there were a number of people of basically republican and radical sensibilities, for example Léon Blum. The Dreyfus affair was very much the catalyst that made French socialists realize that they believed in human freedom and dignity even more deeply than they believed in the class struggle, though such an admission could never be made.

The Millerand affair of 1904 highlighted another breach in socialist ranks, the issue again being, in part, republican defence, though to this was added the question of participationism. Millerand, a well-known representative of the revisionist wing of French socialism, had been responsible for the St. Mandé programme, accepted by the socialists in the 1896 congress. The programme, one of the classic statements of revisionist socialism, defined three elements necessary to characterize a socialist programme: firstly, intervention of the State to 'convert from capitalist into national property the means of production and exchange *in proportion as they became ripe for social appropriation*'; second, conquest of governmental power *through universal suffrage*; and third, the creation of an international *entente* of workers—though socialists, Millerand claimed, were patriots as well as internationalists, and had never had the 'unnatural and insane idea of destroying that incomparable instrument of material and moral progress; the French fatherland' (Ensor, 1908, pp. 49-55). Guesdists had reacted to this programme with the reasonable claim that it contained merely radical ideas clad in socialist phraseology. In 1899 Millerand, in the spirit of the St. Mandé programme, entered the Waldeck-Rousseau (Radical) government which had been set up in the face of the threat from the Right to the Republic, instigated by the Dreyfus affair. Guesdists, apart from their distaste for the idea that Millerand should sit in the same cabinet as General Gallifet, 'the Massacrer of the Communards', held that it was no job of socialists to co-operate parliamentarily with bourgeois elements at all: this was not permitted by the class struggle, which was the very basis of socialism. Participation meant violation of fundamental doctrine and dilution of working-class solidarity, and augured ill for internationalism. Jaurès and the reformists on the other hand saw participation as logical, given the presence of socialist deputies in parliament, and believed that socialists should use the system to wring reforms out of the bourgeoisie. These arguments, though well rehearsed in most socialist parties at this time, have been cited here as evidence of two clear characteristics of the French Socialist party over the past fifty years: its revisionism and its radical-Republicanism.

In the 1920's after the split at the Tours Congress when 130,000 out of the party's 180,000 members (though significantly only 13 of its 66 deputies), quit revisionism and voted to rename the party, *Parti communiste français*, depletion of numbers and dilution of doctrine combined to point the S.F.I.O. towards an alliance with the Radicals. Thus in 1924 the S.F.I.O. formed the left-wing of Herriot's *Cartel des Gauches*. The party became progressively 'radicalized', and this process was demonstrated by the election of Léon Blum at Narbonne, an old Radical stronghold in the south, in April 1929. The party began to replace the Radicals in the agricultural south, where the voters were less likely to be voting for Marxism or reform than for Republicanism, their enthusiasm for which they could demonstrate by voting for the candidate *le plus avancé* (Micaud, 1963, p. 194). Inevitably the party was influenced by the new following gained from the inroads it made into the old strongholds of the declining Radical party in the inter-war years, but it remained the prisoner of its Marxist tenets and continued to use its revolutionary symbols (Williams, 1964, pp. 94-5). It was this ambiguity and ambivalence of orthodox principles and reformist leadership —of class-war dogma and faith in liberal democracy; of opposition to the bourgeois régime and co-operation with the bourgeois parties; of internationalism and patriotism; of revolution and peaceful change—that gave the S.F.I.O.

12

a confused sense of mission and a blurred electoral appeal. Throughout this period, unity was preserved only at the cost of individual defections and splits, as evidenced in the mass revolt of 1920, the breakaway of the nationalistic and neo-fascist group led by Marcel Déat in 1933, the split between the collective security/anti-appeasement group (Blum and the leadership) and the pacifists (general-secretary Paul Faure and half the membership), and, most seriously of all, the split in 1940 when over 80% of the party's parliamentary representatives voted in favour of giving full powers to Pétain.

National inheritance

Added to the traditional dilemma, common to most socialist parties on the continent, which these splits reflect, the S.F.I.O. suffered from a strategic dilemma which was the product of French history. Traditionally French politics have suffered from a basic lack of consensus on fundamentals. The parliamentary system has never received unanimous endorsement from the parties, and there have existed very large extreme left- and right-wing forces which have traditionally rejected the democratic solution; so strong were such forces in the Fourth Republic, that in 1951 they (the P.C.F. and R.P.F.) secured almost half the total votes cast in a general election. Between these two extremist poles of reaction and revolution were the democratic forces who accepted the rules of the game, and who, in the light of the anti-parliamentary and therefore anti-republican threat from extreme Left and Right, saw their prime function as the defence of republican institutions. As Dr. Queuille, one of the premiers of the Fourth Republic, stated: 'Nous sommes condamnés à vivre ensemble.'

The polarization of revolutionary Left and counter-revolutionary Right, symbolizing the struggle between

13

equality and authority at the expense of liberty, was a direct expression of the self-nurturing and self-perpetuating dialectical confrontation of reaction and revolution, instituted by the French Revolution. The Jacobin egalitarian outlook of the Left stiffened the élitist and authoritarian values of the Right, this essentially philosophical conflict being reinforced by the class conflict generated by industrialization. It was a process that produced a dilemma for all parties of the democratic consensus; most commonly, it had the effect of driving them into coalitions where they were forced to compromise with each other for the sake of republican defence. Governments of this type, dominated generally by Radicals, who are traditionally the group most skilled in the process of compromise by virtue of the fact that they possess few fundamental beliefs to inhibit such a process, ruled over France for most of the period of the Third and Fourth Republics. The essential weakness of such centrist coalitions was, of course, their lack of fundamental unity, such arrangements being no more than reactions against one or other or both of the two political extremes. These coalitions, rent by such feuds as the clerical—anti-clerical one (M.R.P. against S.F.I.O. and Radicals), or the disagreement over economics (M.R.P. and S.F.I.O. against Radicals), have lacked the necessary degree of homogeneity or cohesion to tackle the serious economic problems which faced France. Because of this inbuilt impotence of the 'democratic', or republican, parties, there has been a tendency for extremist reactions to such centrist coalitions to develop. Hence in 1935 the centrist parties were forced to enter into a popular front with the P.C.F. to defend France from the fascist reaction, and in 1958, when the threat of an authoritarian régime to free France from the immobilism of the *système* posed itself, the centre parties were faced with the dilemma of deciding either to support de Gaulle, or to forge an

14

alliance with the P.C.F. against him and the dangers further to the Right. Fundamentally, the demoralizing factor in this process has been that the issue of republican defence, overshadowing all others, dictated political alignments that did not lend themselves to successful adjustment of economic or social problems, or to the maintenance of the doctrinal integrity of the parties.

The impact of such a system upon the Socialist Party has been profound. The party was conditioned to wage war on two fronts: against the Communists on the one hand, with their hold on the majority of the French working class, and against the petit-bourgeois anti-statists of the Right on the other. Because of this situation the party could only exercise power through a coalition, which it did with the party closest to it in spirit, the Radicals. Electorally fruitful, such alliances tended to break down in parliament when the lowest common denominator agreements on policy were seen to be so empty of substance, and indeed were limited to such hard-worn causes as anti-clericalism and republican defence. The Popular Front, established with great hopes on the Left, was nothing more than a negative alliance against the Right, and Blum kept his word to be the 'faithful caretaker of capitalism'.

The socialist dilemma and post-war prospects

It is clear that the combined effect of a 'radicalized' S.F.I.O., orthodox in ideology, revisionist in tactics, and the profound strategic dilemma imposed by the peculiar balance of political forces in France, has been that the party has had little freedom of manoeuvre, and that its policies and performance must be evaluated in the light of this situation. It has been unable to appear as a reformist party and deny working-class solidarity because this would cost it the support of what few industrial workers still vote for the party (20% in 1951), and it would be opposed by the party militants who have traditionally favoured Marxist slogans. But equally, to carry the revolutionary programme to its logical end would precipitate a dangerous, and pathologically unwanted, alliance with the P.C.F., which would be able to out-do the S.F.I.O.'s revolutionary fervour, and into which the socialists would thus be subsumed. On the other hand, it was equally crucial for the S.F.I.O. not to lose the votes of the liberal or Jacobin petit-bourgeoisie, whose support it had increasingly gained by its stand on republican issues such as the Dreyfus affair and support for French involvement in the First World War, and who had a strong antipathy to Marxist theory. Hence, the only practical strategy for the party to pursue was to attempt to satisfy both Marxist and liberal followers by continuing to talk of revolution, whilst actually pressing only for specific, mild reforms. Almost half the French population were independent producers, and many of these voted Socialist or Radical : they could hardly be expected to support a planned economy. On the other hand, the same could not be said of the many civil servants and school teachers who have comprised a particularly stable element in the S.F.I.O.'s electoral support. A heterogeneous following could not be sacrificed for the sake of ideological purity.

Immediately after the war, the party's prospects seemed to improve. It had a good Resistance record; parliamentary democracy and political freedom, for which it had traditionally stood, had recovered prestige, and many pre-war anti-socialists stood discredited by their record since 1940. Furthermore, there was widespread recognition of the need for social reform. Yet despite all this, the S.F.I.O. still found itself imprisoned, sandwiched between the two parties which emerged on its left and right flank respectively after the war, the P.C.F. and the M.R.P. Throughout the three years of tripartism (1944-47) which was an alliance born of the Resistance, the S.F.I.O. was reduced to a fate similar to that of the British Liberal Party: by co-operating with the P.C.F. in 1945 it suffered defections to the anti-Communist parties, whilst by collaborating with the M.R.P. after 1946, it suffered the defection of anti-clericals. But any alternative course of action was not clear. In the wave of anti-Nazi feeling after the war, anti-Communism, especially in the light of the noble record of Communists in the Resistance, was impossible: yet no S.F.I.O.–P.C.F. coalition could survive without the socially and economically progressive catholics (M.R.P.). With the ejection of the Communist ministers from the *tripartiste* government in 1947, and the shift in French politics to the Right which that event both symbolized and provoked, the S.F.I.O. increasingly became the prisoner of a conservative majority, too weak to impose its own policies, and able only to work with the M.R.P. to prevent the dismantling of their post-war reforms. The party was forced to tolerate this unenviable position because without the S.F.I.O. there could be no republican majority, and the alternatives to such a centrist or third force majority were the R.P.F. or the Communists.

The S.F.I.O.'s dilemma—to retain office in governments it disliked, whilst alienating many of its rank and file who retained an emotional commitment to revolutionary slogans—produced serious dissension, to which also the party's progressively poor showing in elections contributed (electoral support fell from 24% of the votes in 1945 to 18% in November 1946, and 15% in 1951, 1956 and 1958). At the Lyons Congress in 1946 the rank and file led a purge of the 'revisionist' leadership, which involved the unseating of the general secretary, Daniel Mayer, who was replaced by the then 'orthodox' Marxist, Guy Mollet.

17

Mollet and the orthodoxists successfully resisted the attempt to revise the party's doctrine (Graham, pp. 198-200), and attempted to pull the Socialist deputies out of the third force government, but not surprisingly found that the traditional tendency for the party to be represented in the National Assembly by radical-revisionists, men skilled in, and in many cases given over to, the arts of political compromise, made it impossible for him, even with the support of the Congress and the *Comité directeur*, to get his way. As the Cold War hardened in the late 1940's however, Mollet progressively dropped his Marxist stance and joined the ranks of the participationists. He came to endorse the traditional revisionist claim that preservation of the parliamentary Republic involved participation, even if at the cost of the party's programme and popularity (see also Williams, 1964, p. 90).

Any study of the Socialist Party's policy would be unavoidably two-dimensional were such factors not taken into account. A party with a divided ideological inheritance, though slipping perceptibly further into radical habits of thought and action, and a party enclosed, by virtue of its commitment to liberal democracy, in a situation from which it could not break free, was one whose policy commitments inevitably took on a certain predictable ambiguity. It was a party with a fatefully ambivalent ideological legacy and one for which circumstances alone raised innumerable problems (see Lockwood, 1959 and Macridis, 1960).

3

The S.F.I.O. and internationalism

The post-war mood

The Liberation saw the triumph of the Left in France.
During the Occupation many socialist leaders had become
prisoners of a revolutionary myth which was to cloud
their judgments of post-war political realities (Graham,
p. 39). In their somewhat simplistic analysis, the Right was
seen as having, under Vichy, identified itself totally with
fascist reaction and the German enemy. The Left, it was
argued, could not but fail to benefit from this self-discredit-
ing of the Right, for the French people had come to
accept the inevitability of socialist revolution as the means
of restoring national self-respect and sweeping away the
reactionaries. (The *tripartiste* coalition which ruled France
from 1944-47 reflected to some extent this mood of high
expectation on the Left.) With great enthusiasm the socialists presented the S.F.I.O. as having been purged of its im-
purities by the experience of the Resistance and renewed
in its structure and leadership. The men in charge had
risen during the Resistance: traitors and cowards had been
'pitilessly excluded' (J. Moch, *B.I.*, Jan. 1945). S.F.I.O.
leaders proclaimed that the party stood for revolution, in
the Jaurèsian rather than the bolshevik sense, whereby
economic justice would be achieved without sacrifice of

individual freedom. 'Le Socialisme,' proclaimed André Philip, 'c'est l'avenir' (*Le Pop.*, 17-18 Jan. 1944).

This fervour was given added impetus by the desperate economic situation in France. The winter shortages of 1944-45, industrial production in January 1945 running at only 32% of the 1938 volume, an acute coal shortage and a transport system all but broken down, all seemed to justify the S.F.I.O.'s demand for widespread nationalization, yet there appeared little relation between the statement of Robert Lacoste (Socialist Minister of Production) that a 'wider free sector remains the fundamental condition of French activity and economic recovery' (*Le Figaro*, 17 Oct. 1944), and *Le Populaire*'s demand that action should be taken before the capitalists had time to prepare their defences. Despite this inconsistency, and the attempt by the revisionist leadership of Blum and Mayer to lead a formal retreat from the party's commitment to Marxist orthodoxy, Guesdist tendencies had re-emerged in the euphoric period after the Liberation and foreign policy positions taken up by the party in the early post-war years reflected this. For example, one of the party's major foreign policy interests at that time was the re-establishment of the Socialist International. This had widespread support right across the party, but was particularly favoured on the left-wing, strong in the federation of the Seine and led by the neo-Trotskyite, Marceau Pivert. For the S.F.I.O. a stance of this kind was essential for a party which sought to establish its place as the true socialist party of Karl Marx and of the proletariat. It was a reflex to the ever-present reminder, provided by the enormous Communist Party, that the party was nothing of the sort. Yet, for whatever motives, the internationalist theories of the S.F.I.O. are important, because it was by way of such that the party came to achieve an intellectual justification for its progressively pro-European posture in the post-war years.

The left-wing, the 'orthodox' Marxist internationalists, envisaged the restoration of the national economy on socialist lines in the context of a Socialist United States of Europe, which was an aim concomitant with that of reviving the Socialist International. Thus the socialist solution could more than ever be presented as both a national and an international solution. First and foremost, it would be good for France, and, as a factor in the S.F.I.O.'s perpetual feud with the P.C.F., no chance should be lost to contrast the S.F.I.O.'s *French* internationalism with the P.C.F.'s *Soviet* internationalism; and to emphasize, as had been done on many occasions since 1920, that the P.C.F. was a party of the East rather than of the Left. The 'Guesdist' internationalists were inclined to the Marxist view that the 'workers, dispossessed of the soil and of the instruments of their native land, have only one *Patrie*, and that is not contained within the frontiers of one nation, but comprises all the working men of the universe' (Marx, *Socialiste*, 13 March 1866). This belief in an international *entente* of the proletariat was strongly held on the party's left-wing, but this was relatively small and uninfluential. The essence of the party's post-war internationalist theory was not of the 'orthodox' school, but of the more utopian and pragmatic schools of Léon Blum and André Philip respectively.

Blumian internationalism

The position of Léon Blum in the Socialist Party after the war was without equal since the days of Jean Jaurès, and indeed in the pantheon of socialist fame Blum stood second only to the party's founder who had fallen victim to an assassin's bullet in 1914. Léon Blum had led the anti-Communist rump of the party from the *débâcle* of the Tours

Congress in 1920 to the 'triumph' of the Popular Front in 1936. During the war he had been imprisoned by the Germans in Buchenwald, and after it emerged as an almost messianic figure to whose speeches and writings reference was constantly made. It was in fact his famous book, written in Germany during the war and published in 1945, *A l'Echelle Humaine*, which secured for Blum the position of the party's foremost exponent of a brand of humanitarian socialism, strongly reminiscent of Jean Jaurès. It has already been recalled that Blum's joining the socialists was probably motivated more by his horror at the treatment of his fellow Jew, Dreyfus, than by any commitment to socialist dogma. Marxist scientific socialism had never made much impact upon him, as he demonstrated in his abortive attempt in 1946 to shift the emphasis in the party's ideology from *lutte de classe* to *action de classe*, a proposal which was revisionism indeed for a party as devoted to ideological myths as the S.F.I.O.

In his book, Blum envisaged a post-war international order. In doing so he lost no chance of exposing the P.C.F.'s pseudo-internationalism. A party which owed its allegiance not to an international organization, but to another power —a state which changed the orders of its own accord as its own national interests changed (e.g. in 1939)—was not an internationalist party, but a foreign, nationalist party. 'The distinction,' wrote Blum, 'is vital. Internationalism is based on the postulate that among all nations at the same stage of economic development there exist a certain number of common ideals and interests. The activity of an internationalist working-class party is based on the conclusion that if one looks far enough below the surface and far enough into the future, the interests of every country will be seen as inseparable from the deep and long-term interests of the other countries of Europe, and even of humanity itself.' Blum's socialism, which assisted him towards such an interpretation of internationalism, was, he claimed, a synthesis of Marx and Jaurès: from Marx, the dialectical materialism; from Jaurès, the humanizing factor of man's reason and conscience, to influence the inexorable consequence of economic evolution. Socialism was to be the realization and the justification of the glorious watchwords of the French Revolution—'liberty, equality, fraternity'—and through socialism, the 'heroism of the fighters for *democracy* [my italics], whose struggles have filled Europe and the world for a century, will find its highest expression and its triumph'. There is no doubt that Blum felt infinitely more sympathetic towards a socialism compounded of the idealism of the creeds of democracy and human brotherhood, than of dialectical materialism, and this preference is apparent in his conception of the internationalist ideal. For him, internationalism was the ultimate expression of social democratic ideals, but further, and more important, social democracy was unattainable except within an international context: a European order, or, since the war had further diminished Europe's place in the world, a human, or universal, order. Social democracy, involving as it did the transformation of working-class life and control of the national economy, could not be achieved within the limited context of national frontiers. Nation states were unavoidably members of an international community, bound by laws of competition and international trade: the quest for markets required recognition by a state of reciprocal rights, infringement of which would expose that state to commercial, and thus political, penalties. Social democrats had to acknowledge the reality of interdependence: states had either to shut themselves off from the outside world (as Soviet Russia and Nazi Germany had done), or accept the fact that they were no more than parts of the great international community. (This was, in fact, Blum's defence for

23

his Popular Front government having been a faithful care-taker of capitalism: what else could, and one suspects from Blum's revisionist position, what else *need*, it have been?) Interdependence being a reality, the whole conception of national frontiers should lose caste and shed its importance in favour of a supranational organ prepared to legislate on such questions as markets, raw materials and currencies (Blum actually suggested an international currency), and empowered to raise taxes for its own budgetary purposes—the most supreme of powers. Not only did Blum see this as logical, but also as affording a solution to the German problem, by enabling the incorporation of Germany into an international community powerul enough to re-educate, discipline, and if necessary, master her. This latter was a theme which many French socialists were to take up, and must be seen as representing, for a French party, a relatively idealistic and unpunitive attitude towards the Germans. Of all the French parties, the S.F.I.O. was to be the first to drop hysterical anti-German attacks in the early post-war years, and the first to take up a position explicitly opposed to annexation of German territory, for example the Saar (Freymond, 1960, p. 225).

Blum's internationalism represented also an elevation on to an international plane of the social-democratic concept of man's social obligations: narrow clannishness and jingoistic nationalism were essentially the same as selfishness of the individual (Blum, p. 135). Socialism aimed at a universal society founded upon equal justice for all men and equal peace for all nations, an aim involving the enrichment of human personality, and the relief of man's poverty, spiritual as well as material. Convinced as he was of the perfectibility of human nature, and indifferent as he was to the iron-law prescriptions of the 'orthodox' scientific Marxists, Blum expressed in his humanitarian

24

universalism much of the romantic sentimentalism of the
1789 and 1848 traditions. Indeed, in his emphasis on the
significance of the moral forces of the socialist movement,
in his disdain for injustice, and in his unflagging optimism,
Blum must be seen as typical of the socialist of bourgeois
origins (see Michels, p. 241). It was the internationalist
theory of this (Blumian) school, that was to comprise the
essence of the S.F.I.O.'s internationalism after the war.

The theory of the big market

The other important school of internationalist thinking
was represented by André Philip, who like Blum, represented the Jaurèsian, 'revisionist' tradition in the S.F.I.O.,
and, also like Blum, advocated doctrinal reform in 1946.
Elected a deputy in 1936, Philip became Economics Minister in the *tripartiste* government in 1946, a post he held
for two years. One of the party's few intellectuals, he was
forced out in 1957 after bitterly attacking the Mollet
Government's policies in Algeria and the Middle East. (His
expulsion came as a culmination to a relationship between
himself and the Mollet bureaucracy which had long been
uneasy, and by 1959 Philip had severed all links with the
party, and had joined with other, by then ex-S.F.I.O.
members, Edouard Depreux and Daniel Mayer, in establishing the *Parti socialiste autonome*.) Throughout the post-
war period however, Philip became the Socialist Party's
foremost intellectual exponent of the 'European idea'. Like
other exponents of the revisionist case who were trying to
drag the party away from its class-war ideology, Philip
was entirely hostile to Marxism when it was erected into
anything more than a method of socio-economic analysis
(Graham. p. 218), and his interpretation of internationalism
represented a radical revision of Marxist economic theory.
His basic concept (which he re-stated in his book, *Les*

25

Socialistes, 1967), was that of the large market. He believed that only a large market of 200-250 million people, as in America and in Russia, a market with a minimal reliance on imports, could possess sufficient autonomy to pursue independent economic and social policies with any chance of success. The Marxist analysis and prediction had been wrong: the gradual subjection of the whole economy to the process of industrial concentration, with the resultant expansion to numerical superiority of the proletariat, increase in poverty, intensification of the class struggle and the increasing inevitability of socialism with the technological development of productive forces, had not occurred. This fact implied a need for a revision of Marxism; a recognition that democratic socialism was not inevitable and that workers would remain a minority. 'Socialism,' held Philip, 'tends to affirm its idealistic or spiritual character. It does not arise as a mere product of circumstances, but from the will to organize a new society based on a certain conception of the common good; in other words, on a non-economic value' (Philip, *S.I.I.*, Aug. 1952).

From Marx, Philip moved on to Keynes, accepting the view that the taming of *laissez-faire* capitalism by Keynesian techniques had greatly strengthened the argument for economic revisionism. Keynesian techniques, however, were applicable only nationally (they originated as a reflex of a nation to protect itself from disasters of the 1929 type), and Philip believed that national-scale economic planning was no longer possible in view of the dominant position of the American economy, which, by its very size and influence could cause price and capital movements capable of destroying the economic equilibrium of the smaller European countries. The self-sufficiency of the American economy meant that every change in American production lead to a relatively greater change in world prices, in imports to European countries, and in their balance of payments. European states were therefore, according to Philip, reduced to responding by successive and contradictory adjustments to price movements originating in the United States, and this ruled out the possibility of constructing a planned socialist economy in one country. Thus it was that only a unified Europe, closely linked with all its overseas territories, would be able to provide a market which would be comparable in size with that of the U.S., and able to avoid playing a merely passive role in the face of shifts in the balance of payments caused from outside. Such a Europe would also offer the means of technical progress and thus the creation of new wealth and higher living standards.

Such was the essence of Philip's commitment to European integration, which, apart from the mention of a 'planned socialist economy' being an impossibility in any single country, and the possible inference that socialism required a larger stage (though little was made of this), scarcely differed from that of the non-socialist Europeans (e.g. Hallstein, 1962, p. 5). It was, in fact, Philip's thesis of the big market which formed the substance of the S.F.I.O.'s first policy statement on Europe, 'L'Union européenne', in 1949, which argued for the abolition of customs barriers and the creation of a European economic union as the only means by which Europe could maintain and develop its economic strength and its people's living standards; by fusing separate economies and planning production, Europe could attain self-sufficiency and independence of both the Soviet and American blocs, this last point representing a preference for 'third forcism' shared by many French parties in the 1940's.

Socialists and the United States of Europe

In the early post-war years the interest of socialists like

27

André Philip in European unity was expressed in such organizations as *le Mouvement socialiste pour les États-Unis d'Europe*, which did much to propagate the idea among socialist parties. It was partly as a result of pressure from bodies such as this that in May 1948 a *Conférence Socialiste de Paris et les États-Unis d'Europe* was convened by the S.F.I.O., and attended by representatives of 15 socialist parties, the delegates including Dalton (Britain), Buset (Belgium), and Saragat (Italy). The gathering was able to agree on a *communiqué* that 'it will be in the context of the United States of free Europe, a step towards the unification of the world, that the economic, social, political and cultural objectives of the workers of these countries can be obtained'. The conference also drew up a working definition of 'the United States of Europe', which involved a pre-disposition to delegate part of a state's national sovereignty to a European supranational power. The whole edifice was to be founded on such fundamental principles as democracy and the Rights of Man, a definition significantly empty of socialist substance. Similarly pragmatic in essence was a list made of factors held as determining socialist participation in the creation of a United States of Europe: the need for a big market and a combination of resources to enable maximum application of the productive forces; secondly, the need for a third world force to act as a stabilizing element in a world dangerously divided by two big powers; thirdly, a means of settling the German problem by integrating Germany with other states on a basis of equal rights and thus avoiding a restoration of German sovereignty; fourthly, a means by which both fascist and Communist totalitarianism might be opposed; and fifthly, a means of establishing the only political and geographical framework in which socialism could be constructed. The last-mentioned factor was not expanded, and although the conference report con-
28

tained splashes of orthodox rhetoric, it was distinguished by its lack of commitment to what might be determined as specifically socialist objectives. It spoke in fact of a 'free circulation of men and goods' and evidenced a considerable flexibility on the question of ensuring the socialization of the internationalized European industries.

What this conference showed was that in the Spring of 1948 the European socialist parties, among them the French, expressed their faith in European integration as a means of organizing all resources rationally and as a means of creating perpetual peace. Yet, true to their internationalism, if less so to their socialism, the parties were at least anxious to fix their gaze beyond Europe. In Mollet's words, Europe was 'but a step towards world unification', and in the words of the conference *communiqué* 'the European union is to remain open to all nations, East and West'. In such a way the socialists were not only affirming their hope that this Europe would express their desire for peace, social justice and democracy, but that it would also manifest what these specific aspirations implied; a universalism —the truly international order of Jaurès and Blum. In the uneasy months of 1948 it was seemingly still possible for socialists to express this utopian faith in universalism, without tempering it strongly with the anti-Soviet rhetoric which was to characterize policy statements in later years. The enemies seemingly were still on the Right, and although Mollet admitted that the 'European idea' was not specifically of socialist origins, he also believed that socialism, being the only coherent and powerful organized force in each of the European states, was the only force capable of promoting it: 'It is in this sense that Socialism will make Europe.' 1848 was the year of nationalism; 1948 was to be the year of internationalism: Europe today; the world tomorrow.

The French Socialist Party with its Jaurèsian and

Blumian internationalist tradition and with André Philip's exposition of the case for the large market, was able thus, in the light of the essentially reformist doctrine from which such attitudes derived, to direct its energies towards achievement of European integration. That it did not do so with unanimity, however, as the next chapters will show, was indicative of unease within the party; an unease conditioned in part by conflict between rival interpretations of its internationalist theory, themselves the product of a divided ideological inheritance.

4

Third Force or Western defence

The Marshall Plan—origins of economic integration

Writing in the party organ, *Le Populaire*, in October 1948, Léon Blum recognized in the Marshall Plan a catalyst for European unity: he saw the plans for European federation taking on 'an appearance of reality from the moment when circumstances provided a viable base, namely the Marshall Plan and its call for obligatory co-operation between the participating European states'. The presentation of European integration as a natural extension of what was instigated by the American Secretary of State, became one of the principal characteristics of the S.F.I.O.'s pro-European case at that time and was substantiated in the policy statement, *L'Union européenne*, in January 1949 (J. Poulain, *Cahiers du Communisme*, Apr. 1961).

Marshall Aid provided a test of a number of the S.F.I.O.'s reflexes. Did it not represent American imperialism? Would not the economic co-operation recommended between the recipient states be capitalistic? In view of the Russian rejection of the aid, would it not irrevocably divide Europe? Would it not mean the end of the independent Europe, or Third Force, concept? Although certain left-wing elements, represented by Marceau Pivert and François Tanguy-Prigent, reacted in an orthodox way to

31

these questions, it would not be true to claim that the party as a whole showed much more than a theoretical interest in them. Reference to conference reports and to the declaration of principles made by the European social-ist parties at the first Congress of the newly formed Socialist International at Frankfurt in 1951, confirms that the French party was, in common with the others, con-cerned more that the social democratic solution should be international before it should be, in economic terms, socialist (*B.I.* and *S.I.I.*, Apr. 1951). This naturally was not a novel position for socialists to adopt, but the extent of 'revisionist' thinking was greatly affected by two hard realities in the late 1940's. The first was the undoubted need of West European states for economic aid and the second, not unconnected with the first, was the awareness by late 1948 that the wartime and post-war amity between the Western powers and their Soviet allies was a myth to which the Berlin blockade and the Prague coup stood testi-mony. Commentators in *Le Populaire* began to write in the language of the Cold War. As early as the summer of 1947 these realities had come to be recognized and were sym-bolized by the ejection of the Communist Ministers from the government, an event which both expressed and gave momentum to a rightward trend in French politics as in other European states, and was a consequent impetus for socialist parties to adopt further anti-Communist and 're-visionist' positions.

Broadly speaking the decision on Marshall Aid saw the parting of the ways of the left-wing parties. By their re-actions to the offer, the Communist and Socialist Left in effect determined their respective foreign policies for the next decade. The P.C.F. saw it as American economic im-perialism; the S.F.I.O. saw it as the means for restoring France and Western Europe to economic solvency. After the expulsion from the S.F.I.O. early in 1948 of the

'Bataille Socialiste' (a small fellow-travelling group), opposition to the Marshall Plan in the Party was numerically
insignificant, though acceptance of it was interlaced with
certain clear reservations. Over acceptance of the aid by
France there could scarcely be any dissension among
Jaurèsian patriots. At the 1948 Congress, André Philip,
the Economics Minister, explained what everyone knew :
that the severe economic situation in France was insur-
mountable without the aid. As ministers, some of the
socialist leaders saw this as the most compelling justification for its acceptance. Christian Pineau (Minister of Transport), in welcoming the first instalment in May 1948, had
said that but for such interim aid, the French bread ration
would, owing to the bad harvest, be down to 100 or 150
grammes, and that France owed her survival to the United
States (*Combat*, May 1948). It is clear that for a party
whose leadership sought to keep it in power, and which,
as has already been mentioned, had little option anyway,
such preoccupations were paramount.

Philip was anxious, however, as were others, to present
an intellectual justification for acceptance of the aid : to
see the American offer as of noble inspiration and as of
great importance for the construction of European unity.
Speaking at the July 1948 party Congress, he held that at
that time there was no danger of the Marshall Plan being
used for the purposes of American imperialism. With
American opinion as it was, and with the American
administration as it was, there was a sincere wish to help
Europe resolve its problems without compromising its
liberties. Above all, the Plan would allow Europe a period
in which it could ameliorate its economic condition.

Third forcism

The somewhat defensive nature of Philip's remarks at the

33

1948 Congress demonstrated that third forcism, the advocacy of a neutral Europe, non-aligned with either of the two major world powers, was a factor to be reckoned with in the party, though most French parties showed a nationalistically-motivated predilection for third forcism in the late 1940's. Philip went some way to accommodate this mood. Marshall Aid, he believed, would give Europe a period of four years (the aid was to cease in 1952) in which to become economically independent of the United States, 'that is, to develop large-scale modern industries, capable of mass production at competitive prices'. For Philip the danger lay, therefore, not in accepting American capitalistic assistance, but in not making full use of the opportunity presented by the aid, and in the possibility that such an offer might not be made by a different American administration. (By 1948, the Truman administration had lost its majority in Congress to a Republican party which was entertaining thoughts of isolationism.) To Philip, the problem of European economic unification was no longer a dream or an ideal. Marshall Aid afforded the means for its essential achievement by 1952; it was a question of life or death (S.F.I.O. Congress Report, Jul 1948, p. 440). Most opposition to the leadership's position came, as has been implied, from the exponents of third forcism, advocates of which were not necessarily confined to the left-wing. Blum, for example, writing in January 1948, had argued that 'between the United States, champions of individual liberty and the Rights of Man, but where the capitalist economic system conserves all its strength and inhuman rigour, and the Soviet Union, which has destroyed capitalist private property and eliminated all private, civic and social liberties, there is a place for nations that wish to have simultaneously, personal liberty, a collective economy, democracy, and social justice; that is to say, between expansionist American capitalism and

34

imperialist Soviet totalitarianism, there is a place for social democracy, a place for socialism. The third force would serve not as a barrier or buffer between the United States and Russia, but as an instrument of *rapprochement*, of intelligent reciprocation and conciliation' (*Le Pop.*, 6 Jan. 1948). It was left to delegates from the traditionally left-wing Seine federation to express this concept somewhat more emotionally in the Marshall Aid debate : M. Cotereau, for example, attacked the 'liaison' with the American capitalists and with the 'party of the Vatican'. The S.F.I.O. should be 'true to its true character and unite republican, democratic and laicist elements into a force that would exist between the two blocs in order to save the peace of the world' (S.F.I.O. Congress Report, 1948, p. 467). That there was a strong tendency at this time in the party to envisage Europe as a third force is apparent in such speeches, and even Mollet had warned in April 1948 of the danger of Europe being transformed into 'a sort of military and economic vanguard of America' (*B.I.*, Mar. 1948).

Demonstrating the propensity of the S.F.I.O. to profess economic 'orthodoxy', the party's *Bulletin Intérieur* in April 1948 reflected the suspicion of the American offer, which was, it alleged, motivated by the requirements of an 'expansive market-hungry American economy'; 'rav-aged and pillaged Europe constitutes an important recep-tacle for American production'. Even more than this, the capitalist system was seen to be in danger of collapse unless the economy of Europe was bolstered up : the whole fabric of international capitalism was shuddering. 'Rein-corporation of the European market and industry into a world economy centred on the United States; such seems to be the prime aim of world capitalist strategy in 1948.' The United States, it was alleged, sought to *prevent* Euro-pean economic co-ordination since such co-ordination

35

could be used by the British or French to dominate Europe, against American interests, or, equally, it contained the risk of a neutral (i.e. third force) Europe. At the same time, and somewhat typically, this statement of S.F.I.O. policy equally condemned what it saw as Soviet strategy in Europe, which was to incorporate the East European states into the Russian sphere—into 'a hypercentralized economy under a totalitarian bureaucracy'. The national unity of predominantly agricultural Eastern Europe and predominantly industrial Western Europe was being destroyed by Soviet policy. Yet whilst condemning the Stalinist decision to reject Marshall Aid on behalf of all the Soviet satellites and thus irrevocably divide Europe, the document proceeded to *blame* the American Marshall Aid initiative for the hardening of the Soviet grip on the Eastern states, and for the creation of Cominform in October 1947. Not content to leave its expression of doubts on Marshall Aid there, the party statement saw two grave dangers for socialism: the reconversion of publicly-owned industrial plant to the private sector, under the pretext of re-establishing the free circulation of wealth; and the securing of the social privileges of the old bourgeois classes, especially 'the intermediaries who will use the Marshall credits as part of a vast system of black marketeering and gangsterism'. (Greece was cited as a country where this was allegedly happening.)

Such statements in the official bulletin of the party do much to substantiate the impression of how unprepared were the S.F.I.O. rank and file, for whose consumption the orthodox rhetoric of the *Bulletin Intérieur* was intended, to sponsor absolutely *any* form of European integration at this time, and how the most ambiguous and self-contradictory form of words had to be devised by the leadership to represent the considerable reservations of the party militants to the implications of the Marshall offer.

36

At the same time the party, in its reaction to the offer, revealed, as it was to reveal throughout the post-war period, how incapable it was of reconciling its incompatible ideals with political action in the national arena. All French parties had this problem but the socialists more than any other. The party *had* to show suspicion of American capitalism, as much as it *had* to denounce its enemies on the extreme left for the Russian invasion of Eastern Europe. Seen from the party's perennially imprisoned position, the third force concept was a natural escapist haven. Fighting a war on two fronts made the third force Europe a logical, if utterly unrealistic, goal for the S.F.I.O. However, not even a third force Europe was possible without the initial boost of the American aid that would immediately compromise its independence, and in ultimately agreeing to acceptance of the aid the party was reduced, somewhat pathetically, to 'insisting' on the absence of any political or military strings, on the exclusion of 'fascist Spain', and on the ultimate extension of the aid co-operation to Eastern Europe.

However, it would be wrong to ignore the fact that in its statement of concrete proposals for the employment of the Marshall credits, the S.F.I.O. advocated the establishment of 'democratically-controlled European Commissions' for the purpose of creating a European atomic pool, an 'immediate integration of the west European coal and steel industry', and the 'organization of a common economic union aiming eventually at a complete customs union' (*B.I.*, April 1948). (It was also recommended that the sixteen Marshall Aid states should make preparation for a federal parliament which should consider such questions as common citizenship, the removal of frontiers, a uniform passport, and a charter guaranteeing the rights of man.) The party must, in fact, be given some credit for advocating in 1948 what was not actually achieved until nine years

37

later. The European integration implied in the Marshall Plan seemed to have been reconciled with the S.F.I.O.'s internationalist spirit. The restriction of the co-operation to sixteen countries did not seem to cause distress and the doubts voiced about the economic means by which the 'capitalist' aid would be employed, though important, did not precipitate a division in the Party. Marshall Aid was accepted by the party congress in 1948, which gave Philip's strongly committed and essentially liberal speech an enthusiastic reception. The issue had tested the S.F.I.O.'s Marxist reflexes, and found them to be secondary to other considerations, namely to the immediate needs of reconstruction in France, and to the construction of permanent European co-operation. Although in theory the concept of a third force Europe persisted, the acceptance of Marshall Aid and the progressively hostile dispositions taken up by the Russians in eastern Europe and Berlin, marking the final end of the tactical wartime alliance between liberal democracy and communism, made such a construction impossible, and implied for the S.F.I.O. the acceptance of a form of European integration which could not be reconciled with that particular interpretation of its internationalist ideal.

The Council of Europe

By 1949 the international third force concept had become totally untenable in the light of Western defence needs, and the party was forced to progressively limit its internationalist goals. The immediate post-war vision of Blum's European order, comprising all the states of the United Nations' Economic Commission for Europe, had, in the face of Cold War divisions, to retreat before the reality of American concern for Western defence, which led irrevocably to the welding of the western European democracies to the American interest. Europe was now Western Europe, and the French socialists' commitment to both orthodox and revisionist schools of internationalism became increasingly compromised.

The establishment of the Council of Europe in May 1949, however, provided visionaries with a slight ray of hope, at the same time giving expression to the party's fervent commitment to democratic popular sovereignty. The Strasbourg Assembly was presented by Philip as the personification of the democratic spirit uniting its member states: 'Europe,' he claimed, 'cannot be guided by experts or by negotiations between sovereign states, but by the expression of public opinion, and it is this that the Assembly represents' (S.F.I.O. Congress Report, Jul. 1949, p. 339). At the same time he regretted the complete lack of any powers in the sphere of economic co-ordination; O.E.E.C., set up in 1948 to co-ordinate the administration of Marshall Aid, was insufficient for the tasks of putting Europe on its feet economically by 1952, the year when the American aid would cease. However, the Assembly, with its arrangement for the representatives of the member-state governments to sit alphabetically according to name, and not in either national or party groupings, was seen as an expression of internationalism. 'It is a revolutionary measure, because Frenchmen will vote against Frenchmen' (*ibid.*, p. 342). Philip also envisaged, however, a party polarization taking form in the Assembly after a time, around what he held to be the two major *tendances*: the liberal-conservative and the socialist. The catholic parties, he felt would gravitate to one or other of these two. Thus, out of the traditional instability of the French political system would emerge a two-party stability in the new Europe. Such a view was indicative of the extent to which an intellectual like Philip had little regard for the anti-clerical shibboleth which this analysis ignored,

39

and which was to be the inspiration of much dissension in the socialist party in the early 1950's when it became clear that the integration of Europe was to be confined to a much smaller number of states than those who signed the Statute of the Council of Europe.

The symbolic representation in the Strasbourg Assembly, the first international assembly in Europe, of the French socialists' commitment to the democratic ideal, so well represented by the freedom of speech at all levels of the party, was reflected in the tenor of the debate at the 1949 Congress, where speaker after speaker advocated popularizing the European idea, to enable the people to feel a greater sense of involvement in the movement. To this end the closest co-operation between socialist parties was seen as essential, and in fact the S.F.I.O. set up eighty regional committees to propagandize the idea and to circulate its policy statement, *L'Union européenne*; plans were also made to work in consort with the other socialist parties' representatives at Strasbourg. The French socialists saw themselves as being good internationalists; they were also seizing the opportunity to combine with their party allies in other European states to form the leading left-wing block in any future European assembly, which, like the Strasbourg one, excluded the Communists. A delegate from the Seine federation, M. Lhuilier, revealed this element in socialist thinking, when he spoke of the party's support for the European enterprise as a means of opposing those on the left 'who do not wish to see Europe rationally organized; that is, the Communists'. He saw it as one of the best issues on which the socialists 'could detach the workers from them'. This was yet another indication of the S.F.I.O.'s preoccupation with its infinitely more electorally-powerful rival and enemy on the left.

THIRD FORCE OR WESTERN DEFENCE

The Atlantic Pact—the rejection of neutralism

If the 1949 Congress accepted the Council of Europe's limitations without much demur, the same can also be said of the party's reaction to the setting up of NATO. Like all socialist parties, the S.F.I.O. contained a pacifist element which adjusted uneasily to military realities and to be true to its humanitarian traditions the S.F.I.O. could hardly accept the Atlantic Pact as anything more than a necessary evil. The Party's dilemma was well revealed in Léon Boutbien's speech on behalf of the leadership. 'The pact,' he said, 'is born of insecure climate. Certainly we must not succumb to a psychosis of fear, but it is necessary to know where we are going and why we pursue the method of ratification' (*Le Pop.*, 18 Jul. 1949). Boutbien depicted the concept of a capitalist west facing a socialist east as an over-simplification not corresponding to reality : 'Our fundamental struggle must be directed against the conception of popular democracy prevalent in Russia.' The party had no reason to refuse to ratify the Pact which safeguarded the independence of the democracies. At the same time it was necessary to assist peace and put an end to the Cold War. 'The pact must signify for us the possibility of pursuing East-West negotiations.' Meanwhile, on the left, Pivert spoke of the illogicality of attempting to fight both Stalinism and capitalism and held that the interests of the workers dictated democratic rather than military solutions. 'The only issue for the working class is international socialism and to this end the Socialist International should be re-established as soon as possible' (S.F.I.O. Congress Report, Jul. 1949, p. 458).

Ratification of NATO was for the S.F.I.O. the time to state irrevocably its position in the Cold War struggle. An article written by Mollet a few years later (*Foreign Affairs*, Apr. 1954) shows clearly how committed the

S.F.I.O. was to the Atlantic Pact, and how it saw the relationship between NATO and European integration.
Mollet claimed that the S.F.I.O.'s attitude to world affairs
had a dual base: a 'pacifist' and a 'defensive' approach.
The 'pacifist' approach, founded on the recognition that
the final goal of socialism was universal disarmament and
world peace, emphasized the importance of negotiations
in international organizations to resolve conflicts. The 'defensive' approach (that with which one feels Mollet had
considerably more sympathy), was based on a determina-
tion to 'safeguard peace against the menace of an aggres-
sive force anywhere in the world'. Experience showed that
collective security is dependent on the existence of a force
strong enough to get respect for international order. 'We
see no contradiction between wanting to negotiate and
being determined not to let ourselves be annihilated.' The
free world had to face the reality of Stalinist policy which
was 'universal hegemony'. Socialists believed in the balance
of power, and Engels' comment about 'that formidable
animal, Tsarist Russia, which consents to enter into discussions only with animals its own size', was cited as
vindication of this. Mollet was intent on emphasizing how
much the S.F.I.O. opposed neutralism. 'No socialist will
ever become the accomplices either of those who hate the
United States or the Soviet Union, consciously or uncon-
sciously, but we know how much democracy, in our eyes
the supreme blessing, owes to the courageous American
interventions in the two World Wars. Nor do we forget
that we owe a large part of the material recovery of
Europe to the spirit of solidarity shown by the American
Government and the American people.'

There is no doubt that the party leadership and the over-
whelming majority of the membership were four-square
behind NATO, and the implications of this for any remain-
ing pretensions of a third force Europe were fairly damn-

ing, although Mollet, as late as 1954, was himself still trying to maintain this illusion. There was a clear tendency (as Mollet's article revealed) as the Cold War lengthened, for socialist writers and speakers to emphasize more the issues which, as chapter 1 showed, were the preoccupation of the political, rather than of the economic, left. As the enemy increasingly and exclusively became the extreme left (in France, Stalin's P.C.F.), so the S.F.I.O. tended less and less to speak of the need for Marxist or neo-Marxist economic solutions, which indeed it had never ever done with any degree of commitment, but to take its stand on the defence of democracy. Both in its acceptance of the Council of Europe and the Atlantic Pact, the party revealed this preoccupation with political popular sovereignty. This being its major preoccupation, the party could scarcely avoid the American embrace. The unanimously-adopted international policy motion of the 1950 Congress left no doubts on this score. In a passage which makes an interesting comparison with the January 1949 policy statement, the motion argued that 'the Europe that we wish to build must not try to place itself in a position of impossible neutrality between the United States and Russia. Rather must it be part of an Atlantic community which, having twice saved the world from dictatorship, finds itself today the only defence of democracy and security, and the only means by which the Marshall Plan can be put to use in the evolution of a European economic policy' (*B.I.*, Jun. 1950). The motion further stated the need, at a time when the security of the free nations was threatened, for permanent co-ordination between the United States and Europe, to ensure the most economic application of military techniques. But both in this part of the motion, which reflected to some extent the party's concern to avoid an increased defence burden in France at a time when she was preoccupied with the struggle in Indo-China, and in

43

a reference to the necessity for European integration to be constructed within the framework of an Atlantic Community, so that the relationship between Europe and America would be one of 'fraternal independence', rather than domination by the United States (as it would be were the European states not united in some way), the party was having to recognize the persistence of opposition to the way the European enterprise was evolving, particularly from the pacifist and third-force elements.

If further evidence of the party's somewhat futile attempt to reconcile the international third force and western defence concepts is required, Mollet provided such in May 1950. The general secretary held that it was still possible to create a third force, that it must be independent, but not neutral (sic): 'Dans l'hypothèse d'un conflit, la neutralité n'est pas possible.' The defence of Europe necessitates that she be strong. For that, it is necessary that the countries which compose it abandon a part of their national sovereignty to a European organism. 'A divided Europe will finish by being the prey of bolshevism if we do not take guard.' Not only do these words reveal that Mollet's third force is no more than an adjunct of NATO, they also reveal a significant tendency for the S.F.I.O. leadership to subordinate all else to the defence of the West. European integration, for instance, is required, for this purpose (*Le Pop.*, 29 May 1950).

The bitterness of the S.F.I.O.'s anti-Communism had much to do with the degree of commitment the party in fact displayed towards the Western Alliance. 'Neutralism,' wrote Pierre Commin in January 1951, 'is the way to Communist domination of Western Europe; it is a policy of Stalinists and their tools' (*S.I.I.*, 6 Jan. 1951). It was a socialist minister, Jules Moch, who used troops to put down the Communist-led strikes in 1947, and in 1952 when there were anti-Ridgeway riots in Paris, the S.F.I.O. supported Pinay's Government in breaking up the demonstrations and arresting some of the top Communist leaders (Codding, *Orbis*, Winter 1961, p. 486). This deep animosity possibly did more than anything else to determine the strength of the S.F.I.O.'s actual commitment to Western defence. At the same time acknowledgment must be made of the party's perennial lack of freedom of manoeuvre within the French domestic political context. It could not escape its *damnosa hereditas*, which involved it in stances hostile to those forces outside the democratic consensus. Furthermore, by 1949 the 'European idea' had come to bear the double mark of constructive internationalism and anti-Communism governed by fear, and the form and proportion of these feelings varied within the party with the evolution of the world situation.

5

The Europe of the Six

The Schuman Plan

By 1950 proponents of the concept of a United States of
Europe, in many parties, had come to realize their over-
optimism. It was clear that more limited steps (limited
geographically and substantively, yet still specific in their
objective) were necessary. It was thus that the functional
community approach originated. Functionalism was seen
as a means to piecemeal supranationalism; a gradual limitation of national sovereignty. André Philip, speaking at
the Strasbourg Consultative Assembly in 1951, depicted
the plan proposed by Robert Schuman (M.R.P.), French
foreign minister, as the model for other functional forms
capable of extension to such areas as power, transporta-
tion, labour and agriculture. Philip saw these separate
functional institutions as leading to European integration
and emphasized the need for them to be responsible to a
democratically elected assembly. He saw functionalism
thus as a gradualist approach to eventual European federalism (see Philip, *The Schuman Plan*, 1951), and in so far as
the S.F.I.O. had a clear opinion on detailed provisions of
this kind, functionalism did appear to replace immediate
federalism as the party's official policy. Later speeches by
Mollet reinforce this impression. The plan would immedi-

ately provide a common basis for economic development and be the 'first concrete base for the functional integration of Europe' (*Le Pop.*, 10 May 1950), but its prime inspiration, and to the S.F.I.O. as to most French parties, its essence, lay in its desire to contain the progressive economic recovery and the increasing political autonomy of West Germany. There is no doubt that it was this aspect which consumed the S.F.I.O., though, along with the other 'European' party, the M.R.P., it also presented a positive defence for a Franco-German *rapprochement* within the structure of a European institution.

In *Le Populaire*, the day after the Plan was announced, the headline proclaimed a 'Franco-German iron and steel condominium; such is the essence of the French proposition revealed yesterday' (*Le Pop.*, 10 May 1950). It had the undeniable value of irrevocably engaging the enormous industrial resources of West Germany in the Western community and thus removing the classic causes of conflict. 'The projected organization will serve nothing but the works of peace, in that the Ruhr will cease to be the arsenal of Germany.' Soloman Grumbach, the S.F.I.O.'s spokesman on German affairs, though not a man of great influence in the party, had spoken forcibly in the 1949 Congress for the integration of West Germany into all European organizations, with the clear exception of military ones. (He also stipulated that when he spoke of Germany it was of West Germany solely; a further sign of the socialist acceptance of Cold War realities.)

At this Congress, the question of the internationalization of the Ruhr, forerunner of the Schuman Plan, had also been discussed. In general the idea was welcomed provided that it did not mean a restoration to power of the ex-magnates who had supported Hitler. Many militants professed commitment to the economic integration of West Germany in Western Europe, but maintained an obvious

47

feeling of distrust of Germany and of Adenauer (Mollet, *Le Pop.*, 26 Apr. 1950). Philip drew attention to this paradox. Both he and Grumbach revealed a pragmatic view on the question of socialization of German industry, the former holding that nationalization would be no guarantee against the use of industries for military manufacture, and the latter, that the Allied authorities were unlikely to accept it. An ensuing debate on the question of decartellization revealed how pragmatic the party's position was on this question also. A left-winger, Piette, reflected some dilemma. He advocated the need for decartellization in Germany, but expressed doctrinal reservations, which confirmed the extent to which 'bourgeois' socialist thinking had merged with purist liberal laissez-faireism and how much Marxist economics coincided with capitalist practice. 'The problem of decartellization always poses itself for a Marxist, because the law of historical evolution leads to the concentration of big masses.' Against this Marxist soul-searching, Grumbach put the revisionist liberal case (or was it the truly anti-capitalist case?) in favour of complete decartellization and the consequent curtailment of overpowerful capitalists.

Philip steered adroitly between these two currents by saying yes and no: yes, cartellization was good and inevitable in one instance, and no, it was bad and not inevitable in another. The case for or against cartellization depended on the categories of industries under consideration. There were, claimed Philip, some groups of industries in which the construction of a cartel would be artificial; in these cases it would be necessary to have machinery for breaking up cartels and re-establishing free capitalist competition (sic). On the other hand, there were some industries, for example, the big primary industries, where technical conditions rendered cartellization both inevitable and necessary, though in such cases all the major decisions of

48

economic policy should be in the hands of a European organization (S.F.I.O. Congress Report, Jul. 1949, p. 437). Philip's approach was at least the most honestly realistic. His advocacy of the party's European policy had always been remarkably free from reference to the party's catalogue of shibboleths, but to carry the party militants, who had habitually thought in traditionalist symbols, the official reaction to the Schuman Plan had to include certain conditions: for example, that control of the Franco-German condominium be such as to prevent the reconstitution of a private steel cartel under ex-Nazi industrialists; that the controlling authority should include workers' representatives, and that it be responsible to a European assembly; and that an effort be made to secure the adhesion of as many European nations to the Plan as possible, 'in particular Great Britain, without whose presence the proposition risks taking on the character of an alliance limited to a few states, which will be ultimately directed against others' (*Le Pop.*, 13-14 May 1950). Each of these conditions expresses different aspects of the S.F.I.O.'s tradition: its socialism, its profound belief in popular sovereignty, its 'French' fear of Germany and its idealistic regard for Britain. It is interesting to compare the S.F.I.O.'s 'conditions' on the Schuman Plan with those defined by the Socialist International in September 1952, which emphasized the need for the maintenance of full employment, preservation of national rights to nationalize coal and steel industries, and the issuing of monthly reports on workers' living standards, migration of workers and unemployment —a significantly more 'socialist' list of conditions than those of the S.F.I.O.

Anti-minimalism

If fear of a resurgent German economy not firmly wedded

49

to the West was the basic motive for S.F.I.O. acceptance of the Schuman Plan, it was also the cause of certain misgivings. As was to be re-emphasized during the E.D.C. debate, the S.F.I.O., along with other French parties, feared being left alone with a resurgent Germany and for this reason wanted the assurance of British participation in the Schuman Plan.

There were clear indications that from the announcement of the Schuman Plan onwards, and particularly after it became clear that only six European states would be participating in it, and four of those minor in terms of economic power, that S.F.I.O. leaders, most significantly Mollet himself, began to emphasize the limitations of a Europe of the Six, and particularly of a Europe that did not include Great Britain. On 5th November 1950, the party's National Council declared its conviction that European unification realized without Britain or the Scandinavians would be 'sans valeur' (B.I., Nov. 1950). Speaking in the Consultative Assembly at Strasbourg in August of the same year, Mollet had said that to construct a continental Community on a federal pattern was to cut off all links with Great Britain, and that to establish special links between six countries outside the aegis of the Council of Europe was to put those countries in a virtual state of secession (Philip, 1967, p. 144). Mollet's desire for the British presence seemed to be leading him to a position where he preferred confederal to federal European institutions if such institutions were more likely to induce British participation. He substantiated his reservations in October 1952 by resigning from a sub-committee of the Coal and Steel Community over what he alleged were its increasingly 'minimalist' tendencies (see Haas, 1958, p. 400).

Mollet held that once the conception of Free Europe had been adopted the question became : should co-operation between the peoples of Europe take place in the

framework of a federation (implying a certain relinquish-
ing of sovereignty by all participants), or by means of the
more traditional method of intergovernmental action?
British and Scandinavian attitudes were opposed to the
purely federalist approach, but the intergovernmental alternative was insufficient to solve the economic problems, and
especially to make possible the inclusion of Germany in a
united Europe. Hence a new choice posed itself. Integration
would be by means of a 'geographical' community, uniting
a limited number of nations and without any limitation of
powers, i.e. a federal solution, or 'specialized' communities,
each for a special field (coal, agriculture, transport, etc.),
i.e. a functional solution. Mollet claimed that European
socialists had long opposed the idea of a united Europe
composed of a restricted number of federated or confederated states. On the other hand they had accepted the
principle of specialized authorities provided they fulfilled
two conditions: that they remain open to the largest possible number of entrants, and that they establish close
links of association with states outside.

This was a policy unsympathetic to the purely 'Little
European' policy of some, for example claimed Mollet, the
Christian Democrats. Powers of the new communities
should be real, but limited, so as to enable new states to
join in the course of time. The conception of a 'Six Nation
Europe' (of a 'geographical' community) however, was re-
vealing itself in the demand that signatories of a particular
treaty should commit themselves in advance to a renuncia-
tion of sovereignty, which in fact destroyed the chances
of associate membership, as well as deterring some states
(e.g. Britain) from joining.

Mollet resigned because he saw the E.C.S.C. sub-committee, on which he was serving, attempting to extend
the powers of the Community beyond those laid down in
Article 38, to financial, monetary, economic and social

spheres and to the Saar and Trieste problems. The danger, as he saw it, was the creation of a six-state federation. He resigned therefore, to show what he claimed was the opposition of European socialists to the idea of a united Europe composed of a restricted number of federated or confederated states. The 'Six Nation' approach, minimalist in terms of the number of member states, though maximalist in its content, would lead to the collapse of the European enterprise and to the breakdown of the specialized authorities. For claiming this, he realized he invited the charge of being an 'anti-European'.

Anti-clericalism

The most significant part of Mollet's explanatory article in the Socialist International bulletin was, however, a passage in which he wrote:

> It is not impossible that in the Catholic ranks, the possibility of a grouping of Continental countries with strong Roman Catholic influence, is looked upon with sympathy. I should like to make it clear that I do not believe there exists a compact, united coalition ready to pursue what might be called a 'Vatican policy'; fortunately a number of Christian Democrats have a firm enough conviction as regards the national interest and social progress, not to lend themselves to such a game. But I may nevertheless be allowed to draw attention to the grave injury which some of them are inflicting on European unity by facilitating the division of Europe into two groups, one corresponding to the Protestant and the other to the Catholic sphere of influence (Mollet, S.I.I., 29 Nov. 1952).

This marked the first time that anti-clerical arguments were formally summoned to aid the leadership's exposition of European policy. Soon after, Jules Moch, writing in

May 1953, also referred to 'this little Europe of the Six, that is to say the Holy Roman German Empire resuscitated 1,300 years after Charlemagne and Louis the Debonair' (Poulain, *Cahiers de Communisme*, 1961).

Anti-clericalism had traditionally been strong amongst the militants of the S.F.I.O. For them, the shadow of the Vatican, of the re-imposition of clerical tyranny in France, still rendered the M.R.P., although a socially progressive party, highly suspect. As one commentator has put it:

> Over the Catholic schools the Socialists will admit no compromise: less than ever now that the decline in their industrial following has left them so largely a civil servant's party. The astonishing proportion of teachers among the Socialist leaders (Mollet himself, included), shows why they consider the question of *laïcité* so important. It is a bond between the 'neo-Radical' type of deputy and the most intransigent of the provincial militants, for in the countryside it is the question that counts, and the Socialists depend electorally upon the rural school-teacher as much as the M.R.P. relies on the *curé* (Williams, 1958, p. 74).

It has been common for socialists to vote for anti-clerical right-wing candidates (even Gaullists) in preference to M.R.P. candidates. Specifically related to Mollet's usage of this old socialist issue in 1952 was the fact that in the 1951 election the S.F.I.O. emerged as the Party that had become first and foremost the defender of *laïcité*. There were, as Williams points out, only eight constituencies out of the 105 that the S.F.I.O. won, in which the party's vote did not fall, and in six of these it was fighting alone, without the embarrassment of clerical allies.

It was on the issue of close collaboration with the M.R.P. that the Blum-Mayer suggestion for a French Labour Party, modelled on the British Labour Party, foundered in

53

1946. It was the reappearance of the schools question in the form of socialist hostility to the *loi Barangé* in 1951, that precipitated the S.F.I.O.'s withdrawal from the third force coalition in that year. Later, in 1965, it was ostensibly also on the question of collaboration with the M.R.P. that Mollet refused to accept Defferre's idea of a left-centre electoral coalition, to support his bid for the Presidency in that year. It may be reasonable to argue, especially in the last case mentioned, that certain elements in the leadership have been prepared to use the anti-clerical issue as a means of safeguarding their personal positions in the party, but be that as it may, the fact that the issue is usable at all reflects the great impact it can still have amongst the party's activists, especially in the provinces and the old Radical areas in which the S.F.I.O. gained support in the 1930's and 1940's. The resilience of the anti-clericalist stance of the S.F.I.O. was due in no small part to the party's 'Radicalization' over these years.

The anti-clerical issue has thus undoubtedly been a force of great importance in the S.F.I.O. and there is strong evidence that the reservations expressed by the party's leader in 1952 to the Europe of the Six were based on anti-clericalism rather than anti-capitalism—a force in the party which 'Radicalization' over the years had in fact correspondingly weakened. Mollet's aversion to the 'little Europe' and his strong insistence on the British presence can only be explained in terms of a desire to have a counterweight to the possible Catholic majority and to possible German domination. Economics, beyond the general French fear of competition, common to most parties, were essentially not at issue. 'On the question of the economic integration of Europe, the S.F.I.O. was not divided' (Fauvet, in Lerner and Aron, 1957, p. 129).

During the debates in 1954 on the E.D.C. issue, more evidence of the anti-clerical hostility to the development

54

of European integration was provided by an article in the left-wing socialist journal *France Observateur*, which in May 1954, drew attention to the probable dispositions of the parties in any Parliament of the Europe of the Six. Based on the most recent elections, Claude Bourdet had worked out that the dominant group would be the Christian Democrats with 30 million votes. Socialists would number 15 million votes, Communists 12 million. Radicals and Liberals 5 million, and sundry right-wing groups 16 million votes. The possibility of a left-wing democratic majority was impossible from these figures and the danger of a Christian Democrat-right-wing grouping threatened to create what Bourdet was prepared to call a 'Salazarisme européen' (*Fr.Ob.*, 27 May 1954).

Nevertheless, despite this reservation, the S.F.I.O. maintained its unity, both in its Congress and in the National Assembly (one dissenting voice), and, in December 1951, ratified the Treaty of Paris, establishing the European Coal and Steel Community. It was the largest pro-European party group in the Assembly, its 105 votes being essential to the success of any European enterprise, more particularly since the 1951 elections which had seen the weakening of the M.R.P. and S.F.I.O. and a strengthening of the parties most hostile to the 'European idea'. In the ratification debate, Marcel Naegelen declared on behalf of the S.F.I.O. group: 'The Socialist group will give its support, not to the policy of a government with which it does not always fully agree, but to the great European policy to which France is pledged, and therefore to the E.C.S.C., for which she has, and must keep, the credit' (*J.O.*, Dec. 1951, p. 9000). Thus the majority of socialist parliamentarians and militants, despite the hostility of certain anticlerical and anti-American neutralist elements, held to a pro-European stance, even if they did so with something less than the passion of the Christian Democrats.

6

German rearmament

The European Defence Community

With the announcement in October 1950, of the Pleven
Plan for a European army, the issue of European integration became entangled with, and in time completely over-
whelmed by, the issue of German rearmament. Three
months after the outbreak of the Korean War, the French
Premier, René Pleven, launched his plan for a European
army to combine the defensive resources of Europe. It
represented a compromise between the hostility of the
French government and parliament towards the remilitarization of Germany and the external pressure (mainly
American) for it. It was a compromise between ministers
most opposed to rearmament (such as Jules Moch, S.F.I.O.)
and those resigned to it. It had the merit of substituting
for the emotional term 'German rearmament' the subtler
formula of 'German participation in the defence of
Europe'. The notion of 'Wehrmacht' was changed to one
of 'German divisions in the European Army'. Further, the
principle of equality was to be limited to members of the
proposed Defence Community; thus the entry of West
Germany into NATO, and the restoration of German
sovereignty, would be avoided. It was an attempt to apply
the Schuman Plan method to the settlement of the prob-

lem created by the American demand for German rearmament. The popularity of the 'European idea' was thus harnessed to gain the acceptance of the obviously unpopular remilitarization of Germany. Such was the intent.

Coinciding as it did with national humiliation in Indo-China, the debate in France over whether the E.D.C. treaty should be ratified, constituted the most serious trauma of the Fourth Republic, apart from the Algerian crisis of 1958, the rock on which the Republic foundered. The proposal to rearm Germany, scarcely five years since the end of the third war between France and that country in a lifetime, and with memories still fresh of the humiliation of the Occupation, could only be expected to provoke an emotional response in France; in Aron's words, 'the greatest ideologico-political debate that France had known since the Dreyfus case'.

In the S.F.I.O., hostility to German rearmament had been constantly reaffirmed ever since the War; for example, in April 1950, 'The S.F.I.O. will oppose all policy which would rearm Germany. Neither future and necessary collaboration between France and Germany, nor "integration" of Germany in Europe, can, or must, involve the rearming of Germany' (*Le Pop.*, 29 Apr. 1950). This attitude was explicable in terms of the national fear of Germany and quite understandable from a party with the S.F.I.O.'s strong resistance record. But it was bound, in the light of the necessary construction of Western defence and the growth of European integration, to be challenged by forces in the party favourable to those movements. Indeed, of all the issues concerned with European integration since the War, the E.D.C. issue was the one which provoked the maximum degree of division within the party, and unlike previous misgivings about the integration process in Western Europe, the doubts about E.D.C. were expressed not only in the form of speeches at party

57

congresses, but ultimately by the open refusal of over half the party's deputies to accept the leadership's ruling in the National Assembly. For three successive years (1952, 1953, and 1954), the E.D.C. issue dominated S.F.I.O. congresses, and in May 1954 an additional congress was held in order to decide the party's final position in the ratification debate.

Traditionalist fears

At the 1952 Congress a very clear opposition emerged, in Philip's words, 'animated by an inveterate distrust of Germans, and a general pacifist outlook, which made it oppose all forms of armaments' (Philip, 1967, p. 50). The opposition case had many strands but all tended to converge in one central theme of an entirely emotional anti-Germanism. The most frequent arguments used were that the West German people themselves did not want rearmament, that there was to be no British presence in E.D.C., that it confirmed the 'little Europe' concept, that it would exacerbate the Cold War, and that it finally put paid to the third force conception of Europe. The latter two of these arguments would seem to imply a certain ideological inspiration behind the opposition. Pivert, spokesman for the left-wing pacifist element, argued that 'the Party is forming a foreign policy which has nothing to do with Socialism; of making peace by force' (*Le Pop.*, 31 May 1954). He saw the E.D.C. as conceived in the strategy of bloc versus bloc, thus preventing the creation of an international third force. Pivert represented an element which had been able to accept the Schuman Plan because it bore some hope of acquiring some European independence of the United States. The Korean War, however, had dashed such a hope, and although the Pool had been conceived in the climate of what might be held to be a third force Europe, it became the symbol of the West strengthening itself against the Soviets. Hence orthodoxists who had been able to subdue their doubts over the Coal and Steel Community in 1950 could not not do so over the E.D.C. François Leenhardt's objection was also so inspired. E.D.C., he claimed, was an instrument of United States policy, and the United States had no intention of accepting the third force concept.

It is wrong, however, to see the S.F.I.O. opposition to E.D.C. to any real degree as ideologically inspired. Baser instincts were at work. In the speeches of Leenhardt, Roberte Lacoste and Max Lejeune, particularly the latter two, very clear nationalistic forces were in evidence. Leenhardt spoke, for example, of the unpreparedness of the French people 'to accept the destruction of national armies', and Lejeune attacked the idea of 'denationalizing the French Army'.

The other arguments against the 'little Europe' and the absence of British participation were both manifestations of the anti-German feeling. Lacoste stated that the 'Europe rhénane que l'on nous propose fait penser à l'Europe de Charlemagne'. Hence the Europe of the Six was not only opposed because of its geographical limitation and its possible clericalism, but now, more than ever, because of its strong German flavour. Similarly the desire for British participation expressed, as it had during the Schuman Plan debate, the fear of France being left alone to face German economic competition, and now possible military domination in a 'little Europe'.

The argument that the E.D.C. would encourage similar military policies in the Eastern bloc because of the renewal of the German menace, again reflected this emotionalism of which by far the best exponent was Daniel Mayer, although all the other speakers (Naegelen, Leenhardt, Grumbach and Moch) clearly alluded to it. Mayer was one of the earliest opponents of E.D.C. and by 1954 was one of the most vociferous of the *anti-cédiste* group. 'Le réarmament allemande,' he proclaimed, 'c'est la puissance redonnée aux junkers, aux généraux, aux magnats de la Ruhr.' He claimed that the Germany that was to be rearmed under E.D.C. was not de-Nazified, over 65% of the Bonn foreign ministry staff, for example, being ex-Nazis. A new German army would be composed of the most vindictive refugees from the East. The Europe of E.D.C. would be simply a 'morceau d'Europe'; the exclusion of Britain meant the integration of the German economy into a *morceau* of Europe, or more exactly, integration of the economy of this *morceau* of Europe into the German economy. The arming of the Germans was dangerous because of their avowed territorial ambitions: had not von Brentano demanded the return of all territories held by Germany in 1937? If this was so, Czechoslovakia and Poland, whose territories would thus be seized, would be driven further into the Soviet bloc. 'I would wish that we could show a little respect for the spirit of Czech and Polish resistance to the idea that we are engaged in creating an army with those who wish to dismember their countries' (S.F.I.O. Congress Report 1952, p. 406). Mayer argued that, far from what the *cédistes* claimed, E.D.C. could not be rationalized as a logical step from the Schuman Plan, but rather was it a complete contradiction, since it would recreate the Wehrmacht, the deliberate prevention of which had been one of the central aims of the Schuman Plan's co-ordination of the industries of the Ruhr with those of France and the Low Countries. The Schuman Plan was designed to *prevent* an arsenal reappearing on the Ruhr (*ibid.*, p. 411). Mayer also referred to the lack of enthusiasm in West Germany for rearmament—in the churches, youth movements, trade unions, and most notably in the S.P.D. In claiming that the German working class had thus declared itself opposed,

Mayer's argument appeared to take on an orthodox internationalist caste, but it was in essence xenophobic.

There is, however, some evidence that a few of the *anti-cédistes* were confirmed 'Europeans': Pierre-O. Lapie, for example, who was to be expelled for his opposition to E.D.C., and yet who later became a member of the Coal and Steel Community's High Authority, wrote in 1960 that 'many who were partisans of Europe did not want it built on this sort of foundation' (Lapie, 1960). In August, 1954, Lapie spoke of his objection to building Europe round military aims and claimed that ratification of E.D.C. would kill the chance of creating a healthy European economy.

The cédiste case

The chief spokesmen for the *cédistes*, apart from Mollet, were Félix Gouin, Gérard Jaquet, André Philip, Léon Boutbien, and Albert Gazier. If the *anti-cédistes* manifested an emotional anti-Germanism, the proponents of E.D.C. were inclined to a certain anti-Russianism. One delegate from the Seine federation (M. Bailly) spoke of the need to protect the working class from 'ce poison stalinisme'; Gouin referred to the reality of 'Stalinist imperialism'; and Mollet to the need 'not to underestimate the Soviet danger; Russian policy being to pursue by Hitlerian methods the absorption of one state after another', as evidence for which was presented a catalogue of Soviet territorial acquisitions from 1945, culminating in North Korea (*Le Pop.*, 31 May 1952). The essential argument of the *cédiste* group hinged however on three points: full support, firstly, for the construction of Western defence and, secondly, for the now seemingly fully related objective of European integration, and thirdly, for the complete integration of Germany within both systems.

The speeches of Gouin and Jaquet demonstrated the extent to which the majority of the party's Europeans had come increasingly to regard European integration and Western defence as different aspects of the same phenomenon. Gouin, an ex-Premier and a neo-Radical revisionist from the days of the Third Republic, argued that having obtained political and economic objectives (the Council of Europe and the Coal and Steel Community), there remained the military objective (E.D.C.), which constituted a second line of defence to the Atlantic Pact's front line. Further there should be no forgetting the Americans' sacrifice in 1917 and 1941. Gérard Jaquet, in similar vein, attacked the nationalism of some of the *anti-cédistes* who had claimed that France could not afford increased defence expenditure when she was suffering the drain of blood and money in Indo-China. 'Do you really feel that the Atlantic coalition demands less effort of us than the Indo-China war? The only alternative to the Atlantic coalition is neutralism, and nobody has the courage to come here and advocate that' (S.F.I.O. Congress Report 1952, p. 372).

As on previous occasions it was André Philip to whom was accorded the role of putting the leadership's case. His speeches to the 1952 Congress and to the special Puteaux Congress of May 1954, were, in effect, vigorous defences of the whole European enterprise, and as such revealed the extent to which the entire question of European integration had been put in doubt in the party between 1951 and 1954. 'It was sad,' he said, 'that a Socialist Party had to consider rearmament. The European idea to which a certain number of us have long been attached is essentially a peaceful idea, which is not conceived in the vision of blocs against blocs, but which has given to the people of the West in a context of the solidarity of free peoples, the possibility of an autonomous policy

62

and a common action for peace' (*ibid.*, p. 420). He reiterated his belief that the inadequacy of the nation state
system was total, that is to say, for defence purposes, as
for all else. 'If we continue to work within the structure
of small separated national economies instead of establishing a European economic union under common direc-
tion and capable of permitting the optimum defence,
whilst at the same time assuring social justice and increased living standards, our problems will be serious.
Rejection of E.D.C. will jeopardize all progress made thus
far towards this goal.'

Turning to the German question Philip held that integration of West Germany on equal terms was the only
way of avoiding a recurrence of German nationalism and
of curbing the German menace of which the *anti-cédistes*
had spoken. 'Those comrades who today are opposed to
the E.D.C. are working for exactly the things they seek to
combat, for the alternative to E.D.C. would be German
reunification or the Russian solution of neutralization.
Neutralization will mean a Prague coup in Berlin.' If
Germany was not integrated into Western Europe mili-
tarily she would perhaps look East for a solution. (In
1952 Stalin had offered a re-creation of the Wehrmacht
for a united Germany.) As Gouin poignantly put it: 'If
the German contingents are not in the European Army
they will most likely comprise the first advance of an
enemy offensive.'

'A neutralized Germany,' claimed Philip, 'will also mean
the end of our hopes of a United Europe and all that will
be left for France will be satellite status under the United
States.' The success of the Schuman Plan, and of the whole
European enterprise, depended on full German participa-
tion. German economic strength was required, implied
Philip, and her nationalistic tendencies required diversion.
To the accusation that German integration in E.D.C.

would, as Jules Moch had alleged, compromise chances of negotiations with Russia, Philip held that the only negotiations with Russia that would stand any chance of success were those made from a position of strength.

Mollet, at the 1952 Congress, also emphasized the need for German participation and played on anti-Germanism in the party to gain support for his policy. Nor was he averse to gain support by invoking Franco, the *bête noire* of the left, as an example of one particular species which would never be admitted to any European institution. There were always worse dangers further to the right.

It was, however, necessary for the leadership, in view of the substantial opposition to the E.D.C. project, to devise a set of conditions that the S.F.I.O. would require to be met before it would endorse France's ratification of the Plan. These, announced at the end of the 1952 congress were firstly, the creation of a political authority capable of exercising democratic control over E.D.C., (i.e. with *real, though strictly limited*, powers); secondly, the close participation of Britain with the Community; and thirdly, an American guarantee of full support including the maintenance of troops on the Continent and an obligation to oppose the withdrawal of any member from the E.D.C. The first two of these conditions were very definitely mutually exclusive: the further one went in creating a supranational power the less one could count on British participation. (This is undoubtedly why S.F.I.O. resolutions constantly referred to the need for European organs with 'real, though limited, powers'.) Aron has commented that in these two conditions the S.F.I.O. was symbolizing French vacillation: 'to reduce the risks of German rearmament, they wished the creation of a European authority; but they wanted no part of a European authority in which German dynamism would not be counterbalanced by the British presence' (Lerner and Aron, p. 7).

64

This is very probably true, but it does not entirely do justice to the French socialists who have often demonstrated in the past a regard for Britain that has on occasions seemed like Anglophilia. The tendency is strong on the democratic French left to see Britain as the home of the libertarian ideas which lay behind the French Revolution; and reinforcement of such a feeling was undoubtedly given by the presence in London during the War of many socialists in the Free French Government. Behind the words of Christian Pineau at the 1950 Congress—'for me, as for Jules Moch, the organization of Europe cannot and must not be accomplished without England'—there lay more than the sort of negative motivation Aron has implied.

At the end of the special Congress held in May 1954, Mollet had the somewhat embarrassing task of combating the kind of arguments about 'the Europe of the Six' that he had himself been making in recent years. This theme had been well employed by the *anti-cédistes* at the 1954 Congress; by Leenhardt who spoke of the 'Christian Democratic Europe of the Six, with its doors closed to Britain', and by others who spoke of 'une Europe tronçon, une Europe croupion, une Europe des nations dirigée, dominée par les partis Catholiques, par les partis conservateurs; une Europe cléricale'. Mollet agreed (he could scarcely do otherwise) that the Europe of the Six was not Europe, but nor were the specialized communities representative of the functional approach, a federal Europe. He now seemed to be implying that the gradualist approach was inevitable, but it is very probable that this was merely a rationalization on his part for the real motive behind his change of emphasis: namely, his realization that West Germany should be firmly welded to the Western Alliance.

Writing in February 1952, he had argued that of the two propositions, Western integration or German unification (which the pacifiist wing tended to favour), the former

65

was unfortunately preferable; a united Germany would be a threat to peace, either by playing off East against West or by forming another 1939-type pact with Russia. Priority should therefore be given to Western integration, and that involved placing the Russian danger before the German danger. The supranational concept, involving equal surrender of sovereignty, would be a good means of dealing with the problem of integrating Germany into it. The E.D.C. and E.C.S.C. thus constituted one of the first concrete realizations of European union. Mollet regretted that European unity was being fostered by a defensive arrangement, but held that one had to accept realities and that anyway the establishment of a Defence Community would lead inevitably to measures in all other fields—'a reassuring thought'. Socialists had, however, to bear in mind the need to retain a defensive, not offensive, character for the E.D.C., thus safeguarding the democratic nature of all European institutions and to ensure the democratic liberties of all.

Mollet, however, had clearly compromised his own position somewhat and it is interesting to establish why. There were signs (in 1952) of the S.F.I.O. leadership's desire to placate opposition in its ranks to E.D.C., or at least to appear less enthusiastically pro-European, so as to avoid the brunt of the P.C.F.'s highly successful anti-E.D.C. campaign, which was frustrating the S.F.I.O.'s eternal hope of winning back working-class support from the Communists. This was also a time when the S.F.I.O. was anxious to return to power in a centre-left coalition, and it is certain that Mollet's anti-'Europe of the Six' stance was conditioned in part by this consideration of internal French politics. It was also true that by the summer of 1954, opinion polls were showing that of S.F.I.O. voters, only 35% were in favour of ratifying the E.D.C. whilst 38% were opposed (Philip, 1967, p. 150). On the
66

other hand, such tactics were fruitless since mathematically no centre-left coalition was possible without the M.R.P., which Mollet was alienating by his use of the anticlerical issue. The S.F.I.O.'s strategic dilemma was ever present.

Party split

The division in the party was deep, and it deepened progressively during the two years when successive French governments declined to take the E.D.C. Treaty to the Assembly for ratification. Even in the M.R.P., the bastion of Europeanism, adversaries of German rearmament and left-wing advocates of the third force had to be threatened with expulsion. The first significant rift in S.F.I.O. ranks had appeared on 19th February, 1952, when 20 out of 105 S.F.I.O. deputies (including members of the *Comité directeur*: Mayer, Verdier and Lejeune) refused to support a vote of confidence for the Faure government on an order of the day approving the principle of the European Army. By November 1953, when a debate was held in the Assembly on the general principles of the E.D.C. Treaty, the number of S.F.I.O. dissidents had risen to 42, all of whom had resigned in the meantime from the Socialist Movement for the United States of Europe. At a meeting of the S.F.I.O. group prior to the debate, the hostility of the dissidents to the 'little Europe' concept in the E.D.C. plan was partly met by the deletion of the word 'European' in 'European United Army', and the substitution of 'open to all democratic nations'; but this was not sufficient to quell the rebellion. Greatly exacerbating the division in the party was the *Comité directeur*'s decision to afford the right to speak in the Assembly only to those supporting the E.D.C. Opponents were not even permitted to speak in public on the issue. To invoke party discipline in this

67

case was a serious error since the deep division of the party was a reality which could not be overcome by such tactics.

In late 1953, Mollet showed increasing impatience with the indecision in the party, and claimed that the three conditions they had set down had been met, but agreed that the question be put before a special Congress, at Puteaux in May 1954. Before this, in April, a pamphlet was issued by the Mayer-Lejeune faction, bearing the signatures of no fewer than 59 of the 105 S.F.I.O. deputies. The theme of the pamphlet was an attack on the 'clerical and reactionary Europe of the Six', and it quoted from an article written by Blum in 1949 in which he had argued that a partial European *entente* comprising France, Italy, Benelux and 'l'Allemagne de Bonn' was only desirable with a British presence (*Le Pop.*, 12 Nov. 1949). 'In the E.D.C.,' claimed the pamphlet, 'France would find herself almost isolated; confronted by 85 million Germans and Italians, highly influenced by a clericalism allied to big business. Deprived of the presence of the British Labour Party and left only with the S.P.D., which is hostile to the E.D.C., there is a great risk of the Europe of the Six containing a reactionary majority' (*Fr.Ob.*, 8 April 1954). The nature of the opposition was emotional and unamenable to argument, and its scale was now great. Mollet, however, ignored it and pursued an insensitively dictatorial attitude. His position in the party was so impregnable that the vote on the E.D.C. at the May 1954 Congress was a foregone conclusion; a majority for his policy was assured by virtue of the power dispositions in the party.

The most important element of the S.F.I.O.'s structure is the departmental federation (a grouping of the party's basic unit, the section), which acts as intermediary between the section militants and the higher levels of the party (the National Council and the executive body, the

68

Comité directeur). Delegates for national congresses are selected to represent federations. This has led to great power accruing to the federation secretaries, who have become virtually 'Socialist Prefects', being the officials through whom the party transmits information and propaganda to the local sections and who relay sectional feeling to the higher echelons of the party. As Micaud points out, the departmental federations are thus in a strong position and are used by the central *appareil* by concentrating its efforts on the largest federations (i.e. those with most *mandats* at Congress) to obtain consistent majorities at Congress. This has undoubtedly been the principal means by which Guy Mollet has secured a firm grip on the party's leadership. Since 1946, he has been able to count upon the support of the party's two largest federations, Pas de Calais and Nord, where habits of working-class solidarity persist. Between them, these two northern federations carry 1,000 out of the total of 3,800 *mandats* at party congresses. Next to these two departmental federations in terms of size are Seine, Bouches-du-Rhône and Haute-Vienne, and Mollet had similarly been able to count on the *mandats* of at least the latter two between 1946 and 1958, thus securing the support of over half the *mandats* on most issues in the National Congress. This was the position in May 1954 when in the vote taken on the E.D.C. issue, the Congress voted by 1,969 to 1,215 *mandats* in favour of ratification, a vote which greatly exaggerated the leadership's success, when factors such as the dominance of the two northern federations and the system of mandating delegates are taken into account.

Mollet realized that the victory was hollow, and that the depth of hostility to E.D.C. from the 'Radical' (rather than the small, ideological left) wing of the party, the element strongly represented in the party's parliamentary group, meant that the Congress majority was unlikely to be reflected in the party's vote in the Assembly. Thus the 1954 Puteaux Congress was also called on to vote for a motion 'impressing on the parliamentary representatives of the Party, the absolute necessity of a united vote, in the Assembly and in the commissions, on the basis of the decision taken by this Congress, and that in the event of indiscipline the *Comité directeur* shall be entitled under Article 60 of the Statute of the Party to take all necessary measures to ensure unity and discipline'. This motion was almost more hotly contested than the E.D.C. issue itself, for it posed a direct challenge to the party's undoubted democratic tradition, a tradition reflected in the emphasis upon free discussion on all issues and the convening of special emergency congresses to deal with special issues such as E.D.C. Indeed, it was ironic that it was at such an emergency congress that the party was called upon to oppose further free discussion of the issue. Mayer and Depreux argued strongly in favour of a free vote, referring to the recent decision of the Belgian Socialist Party, a party comparable with the S.F.I.O. in many respects, and which was equally divided over E.D.C., to allow a free vote in the Belgian Parliament. (Of the 76 Belgian social-ist deputies, 29 had subsequently voted against E.D.C.)

Mollet, in demanding a disciplined vote, argued firstly that the demand for party unity conformed with the tradition of the party: 'we are not a party of Radicals, still less of "independents". Already our position taken on E.D.C. is being accepted as S.F.I.O. policy and perhaps we shall be confronted with new elections. We must, in the face of this maintain unity' (*Fr.Ob.*, 28 Jan. 1954). Secondly, he argued that because of the virtually equal division of the National Assembly over E.D.C., it was necessary for socialists to vote unitedly to ensure ratification.

Seen in the best light, Mollet's position seemed to be that E.D.C. was a European issue and that the S.F.I.O., being a European party, should ensure the success of this effort to further European integration. Seen in another light, Mollet's stand on E.D.C., could well have been motivated by a strategy similar to that of the Pleven Government's: to gain French acceptance of German rearmament by linking the question of German rearmament with the more popular idea of European unification. (A poll in May 1953 had shown that 70% of the French people were favourable to the European idea.) In substantiation of this it is possible to refer to the many occasions on which the Secretary-General has emphasized the Party's commitment to Western (i.e. anti-Communist) defence, for if Mollet's career has been that of a 'human weathercock' (*Fr.Ob.*, 18 Sept. 1958), one more consistent strand that does emerge is his resolute anti-Communism. Claude Estier, writing in June 1954, accused the socialist supporters of E.D.C. of being 'motivated less by a desire to "faire l'Europe" than by an almost physical fear of Communism', and Moch had spoken of refusing 'to allow the party to play the role of purveyor of a vast anti-Communist alliance'. These stirrings of third forcism reflect the awareness of these observers that Mollet's personal priorities involved the pursuit of Western defence first, and of European integration second.

In the event, the appeal for unity at the Puteaux Congress produced a vote of 2,414 to 972, though on the part of the motion threatening discipline the vote was 2,484 to 51 (i.e. 900 abstentions). But more than a third (15) of the *Comité directeur* were *anti-cédiste*, and armed thus with theoretical unity only, the party faced the National Assembly debate in August 1954.

Defeat for the leadership

To Mollet's great chagrin, both Jules Moch and Pierre-O.

Lapie, opponents of E.D.C., were able to ignore the leadership's decision to prevent hostile speeches, accorded as they were platforms, by virtue of their presidencies of two of the National Assembly's Commissions. Moch, president of the Foreign Affairs Commission, which had decided against the E.D.C., argued against the claim that E.D.C. would contribute simultaneously to Western defence and European integration, holding that the need for German rearmament to substantiate Western defence had lessened with the easing of Cold War tensions, and that the European integration which the E.D.C. would induce would be that of a 'little Europe', excluding Britain and the Scandinavian states.

It fell to Christian Pineau to make the final speech in the debate, 'in the name of the Europeans', but in the subsequent vote, 53, that is over half the S.F.I.O. parliamentary group, voted for the procedural motion by which the consideration of E.D.C. ratification was rejected. As threatened, the leaders of the rebel group (Mayer, Moch, Lejeune, and Lapie) were excluded 'for their open rebellion against the party'; two others (Lussy and Charlot) were suspended for five years, and the other 47 were suspended for the remainder of the parliament. Intraparty acrimony deepened when the *anti-cédiste* majority took revenge for the harshness of the expulsions by voting Mollet's supporters (Le Bail, Pineau, Jaquet and Gouin) out of their positions on Commissions and replacing them by those of their own number. It is clear that had the S.F.I.O., like the M.R.P., (out of whose 86 deputies only two actually voted against the Assembly considering the E.D.C. ratification, whilst four abstained), voted more unitedly in the Assembly and supported E.D.C., the treaty would have been ratified. There also seems little doubt that had Mendès-France been prepared to make the E.D.C. ratification a question of confidence in his government, the Treaty would also have been accepted, because a reversal in the Assembly for the government would have permitted the dissolution of the Assembly (two crises in eighteen months) and the holding of elections, which Mendès-France's authority in the country at that time would have enabled him to win.

In a statement issued by the *Comité directeur* (*B.I.*, Jan. 1955), immediately after the rejection of E.D.C. by the National Assembly, the party leadership revealed the extent to which its preoccupation was specifically with the construction of Western security. The statement 'deplored the weakness of Western defence which the rejection implied' and 'denounced the manoeuvres of those who seek to put impossible choices before Parliament involving the risk of reversing the traditional alliances of France, the neutralization of Germany and a possible consequent German-Soviet pact'. It also acknowledged the strong Germanophobia of the party, not least of Mollet himself (though his Germanophobia was channelled into, as he saw it, more realistic directions), by emphasizing that the party would never accept in any form a reconstitution of the Wehrmacht, a statement which *Le Populaire* significantly used as its headline on 2nd September 1954. The statement alluded also to the need for 'European solutions' and called for the unity of all 'partisans de l'Europe' to work for the construction of political and economic unity, but the defensive preoccupation reemerged at the end in a final call for the 'maintaining and strengthening of the solidarity of the free nations'. Compared, however, with the other parties, or segments of parties, which had supported ratification of E.D.C., the S.F.I.O. leadership, both in the debates of August and after the collapse of E.D.C., stressed more than the purely repressive aspect of E.D.C. (i.e. its defensive nature and the aim of making Germany harmless). Guy Mollet was one of

73

the few to emphasize the constructive aspect—of how to progress beyond the idea of sovereignty. Differences between states were irreconcilable within a system where state faced state, sovereignty rivalling sovereignty. The one obstacle to the attainment of the Blumian international order was the idea of national sovereignty. It was this idea which, he held, had irremediably paralysed the United Nations by instituting the rule of the veto.

The E.D.C. crisis had nevertheless served to demonstrate just how incoherent was the S.F.I.O.'s European policy. The S.F.I.O., on an issue of European policy, had attained a degree of disunity which was surpassed only in the Algerian and constitutional crisis of 1958. But from his impregnable position in the *Comité directeur*, Mollet was able to devise formulae for reuniting the party and re-establishing, as the *débâcle* in the Assembly on 30th August had shown to be necessary, its European policy.

Reappraisal

Guy Mollet himself had, from the inception of the Schuman Plan, hesitated to choose between two mutually exclusive methods of integration : supranational integration without limits or vetoes, or a looser scheme with full British participation (i.e. with *real, though limited powers*). For a long time the party leadership sought both : for example, in the National Assembly in November 1953, Mollet and Jaquet had protested against the excessive role of the Council of Ministers (the national, as opposed to the supranational, element) in the proposed E.D.C., at the same time as demanding a contract of association with Britain. After the rejection of E.D.C., Mollet showed signs of awareness of the impracticability of pursuing these objectives simultaneously, and increasingly tended to advocate integration limited to the six states if that was

74

the only objective obtainable. 'Unfortunately,' he wrote in April 1954, 'for the time being, Europe, in the sense of a European community formed by the fifteen countries that comprise the continent remains only a hope, though it is still the ideal solution.' Emphasis was also placed on Blum's advice given to the 1948 Paris conference of socialist parties that the European conception should not be allowed to replace the international conception of socialism, the former being but a step towards the latter (*Le Pop.*, 21 Sept. 1954). Mollet himself now displayed contempt for the 'Pas d'Europe à Six', 'Pas d'Europe hitlérienne' and 'Rien sans la Grande Bretagne' slogans. Indeed he went so far as to describe such slogans as Communist-inspired, and no denunciation could be more total in the S.F.I.O. He argued that although the party had consistently, even obstinately, demanded British participation, it was clear that Britain with her history of reserve towards the Continent, her predilection (since 1215) for pragmatic rule without a written constitution, and her general distaste for *a priori* formulae, was unlikely to change her ways. It was clear that Mollet now felt it no longer possible to ignore that the constant demands for institutions of a form appealing to Britain, delayed the solution of the German question, which, for socialists, as for many other Frenchmen, had to be a solution avoiding the restoration of German sovereignty; that is, a solution involving the integration of West Germany into a supranational community, a formula incompatible with the British preference for loosely-associated sovereign nation states.

However, in December 1954, when the National Assembly came to debate the Paris Agreements establishing the Western European Union—the less supranational means by which a German contribution to Western defence was secured—restoration of German sovereignty is precisely what the S.F.I.O. *did* support. Mollet seemed now prepared to forgo all other objectives for the sake of the overriding one, of German integration in a system guaranteeing the security of the free world; in default of supranational integration of the type unacceptable to Britain, and of the type rejected by the National Assembly in August 1954, a military alliance of the conventional type was necessary, and if such involved a restoration of German sovereignty for the sake of the solidarity of the 'free world', then so be it. Naturally enough, Mollet was anxious to reconcile as far as possible his party's supranationalist hopes with the alliance nature of the W.E.U. At least the W.E.U. assembly would comprise a means of 'democratizing' NATO, of creating 'real, democratic control', and further, merely because supranational integration had been frustrated in the military sphere, there was no reason, it was argued, why functional supranational solutions should not be applied to political and economic spheres.

In the vote at the end of the debate on the Paris Agreements of the W.E.U., 18 socialist deputies still defied the leadership, and were immediately disciplined. This group represented a resistant hard core of third forcists and Germanophobes, although since the E.D.C. crisis, many of the *anti-cédiste* Germanophobes had been brought round to the leadership's belief that the welding of West Germany to the western alliance would prevent the reunification of Germany, and the loss of West Germany to eastern influence, this being what many feared above all else. Mollet's speeches at this time, as if to indicate the awareness of these fears, were replete with portentous reminders of Soviet aggression in eastern Europe, the refusal of free elections in East Germany, and the recent riots in East Berlin against the Ulbricht régime. German unification was unrealizable (as well as undesirable) and the essential problem was to 'preserve the liberty of the part of Germany that is still free' (*J.O.*, 30 Dec. 1954).

But for the party's Europeans, the W.E.U. represented an unquestionable set-back; they had had to accept a policy of national sovereignty in the controversial and sensitive field of defence. In Gérard Jaquet's words, 'France to the joy of the nationalists will conserve her army, and Germany can now reconstitute an autonomous force; this, all Europeans profoundly regret' (*Le Pop.*, 1 Jan. 1955). What was now required, he believed, was an extension of functional integration into energy and economic fields, and the election, by universal suffrage, of a European parliament, so as to secure greater popular involvement in the European enterprise. It was in the pursuit of such goals that the S.F.I.O. was to play a significant role.

7

From Rélance Européenne to L'Europe des Patries

By late 1955 there is much evidence to suggest that elements in the party, having shown their reservations about the form integration was to take, had come to accept the reality of the existence of the Europe of the Six, and it was this reality that helped fashion unity in the party. It is also important to note that by the latter half of the decade the powerful myths of the anti-Europeans, for example, the suspicion of Germany and the French economic inferiority complex which clouded the Frenchman's view of the world, and particularly of his German neighbour, were declining in force. The considerable economic expansion since 1953, the discovery by the French that they could compete in many industrial sectors, enabled the discarding of economic fears, particularly those of being submerged by Germany's economic might. The removal also of the issue of German rearmament, and more importantly its removal from involvement with the construction of European integration, also undoubtedly facilitated the forging of a united position.

The Mollet government

Unity was assisted further by the success of the 'Republican Front' parties in the 1956 election, which led to the emergence of the first socialist-led government since Ramadier's in 1947 (excluding Pineau's three-day 'ministry' of January 1955). *Le Populaire* on 31st January welcomed the government with enthusiasm, ('Guy Mollet au pouvoir!') and it is clear that a considerable party effort was made to support this government.

The period of the Mollet government coincided with that of the *rélance européenne*, though the government was not especially more 'European' than its predecessor, the Faure government, which had represented France at the opening of the Messina Conference in July 1955. Any greater commitment to European integration by Mollet's government was to a great extent a reflection of political necessity. The elections of January 1956 had produced a parliamentary situation such that the only possible majority was 'European', owing to the decisive defeat of the Gaullists (Grosser, 1961, p. 245). Mollet's policy statement as Premier-designate on 31st January 1956 should be seen in this light. 'There are some,' he said, 'who voted for E.D.C. without being especially interested in Europe. There are some who voted against it because they were sincerely convinced that it would hinder the construction of Europe. Are we going to behave as if France's international activity had suddenly stopped on that day? Could we be incapable of overcoming past differences in order to devote ourselves to the future? I solemnly entreat the Assembly to stop regarding the European Idea as a subject of disagreement, but to consider it rather as a great bond between us' (Haas, 1958, p. 272). Thus it was that Mollet government's programme specifically included 'construction européenne', involving a common market and atomic pool, and it fell to this government to handle most of the negotiations leading up to the signature of the Rome Treaties in March 1957. But whilst it is true to say

79

that the strongly pro-European forces behind Mollet and others (e.g. Spaak) hastened the negotiations at Messina to take advantage of the existence of pro-European French governments from 1955-57, it would not be true to argue that the Mollet government was especially prominent in the *rélance*, primarily because it was preoccupied with the Algerian war and the Middle East crisis in late 1956.

Mollet had little effective freedom of action. He had to take into account the disparate elements in his majority; most notably had he to respect the opposition of the Mendèsiste Radicals to the Europe of the Six, for whom British participation was a fundamental necessity, and the small Social Republican group (Gaullists) who wanted no truck with supranational institutions. He nevertheless took up committed positions during the National Assembly debates on Euratom (in July 1956) and E.E.C. (in January 1957), though the impression should persist that his motivation in supporting these enterprises was political, in the sense already discussed, and political also, in that he argued a political, rather than an economic defence of the Treaties.

The political case made for the extension of the six-nation integration had in it elements of a resurgence of third forcism : 'Europe with its high tradition of humanist culture has an immense role to play independent of the U.S.A. or the U.S.S.R.' Some speakers spoke of the growing infiltration of American capital into Europe, a trend which the Common Market could resist. But the most common argument, and ironically, the one most difficult for loyal socialists to use, was the isolation and international weakness of France, demonstrated by her humiliation after the Suez affair. That affair had exposed how impossible it was for European nations to initiate action to solve international crises, politically and economically independent of the United States.

Pineau spoke coyly of 'the isolation of our country in the face of certain difficulties', by which he undoubtedly meant the Suez incident, presided over by Mollet and himself, and which had clearly compromised any socialist commitment to internationalist conceptions of the rule of Law. Indeed, André Philip, in the book on account of which he was expelled from the party in 1957, wrote that 'it is a disaster when a government, which calls itself European, presents the European countries with a *fait accompli*; when a government which calls itself a supporter of collective security destroys the foundations of U.N.O. and ignores world opinion; when a government which calls itself internationalist acts contrary to all the socialist parties' (*Fr.Ob.*, 20 Nov. 1956). The humiliation of Suez for the French Government on all these counts was, however, dexterously turned by Mollet and Pineau into arguments for greater involvement in Europe, though indeed it is not impossible that in the light of the Government's disastrous policies in Algeria, as well as the Middle East, the European sphere remained the only possible area in which it could pursue a coherent foreign policy which had any chance of success.

The Treaties of Rome

Whatever the motive, however, Mollet and Pineau submitted the Rome Treaties to the Assembly with impressive commitment. There were signs that the impossible dual objective of British participation and strong supranational institutions persisted: for example, Mollet spoke of his desire not to allow the power of veto in the Council of Ministers (i.e. not to put a brake on the supranationalists), whilst Pineau spoke of 'une petite Europe, ouverte à tous'. This theme of an 'open Europe' began at this time to find expression in the party's call for 'Eurafrique', an internationalist vision of a union of Europe with its ex-colonial empires, reflecting the traditionally strong interest of the S.F.I.O. in the French Union, in many parts of which it had been strong electorally.

Many speakers (e.g. Pineau and Le Bail) were anxious to reassure those with doubts about the economics of integration and indeed to argue that French industry needed the spur of competition. The doubts to be dispelled were not based upon a desire to see specifically socialist planning in the proposed common market, but upon the traditional French fear that the exposure of the heavily protected French economy to the competition of a dynamic common market would be disastrous for French industry which was in the main a system of small producers. It seems likely that this fear, which was one of the most important factors conditioning French reserve of economic integration, was also strong in the S.F.I.O. André Philip has interestingly drawn attention to the possible correlation between the incidence of hostility to European integration and the level of economic development. Thus, support for E.D.C. in 1954 came largely from the federations of the north-east where industry was competitive and would benefit from the reduction of costs produced by the widening of markets, whilst opposition to E.D.C. came from the economically backward regions of the south-west where fear of competition without special protection and a vast overhaul of industry, would aggravate the existing backwardness of the areas (Philip in Lerner and Aron, 1957, p. 31).

Other factors undoubtedly conditioned the demography of the S.F.I.O. enthusiasm for European integration, especially at the time of the E.D.C. debates, but there is no doubt that the S.F.I.O. leadership had occasion to reassure the Assembly of France's ability to compete not only because over half the French electorate were small independent producers, but because a considerable element of support for the party was rooted in economically vulnerable regions. This emphasis in S.F.I.O. discussion at this time was reflected in *Le Populaire*, and especially in a supplement by Professor Robert Mossé introducing the details of the E.E.C. to the Party militants (*Le Pop.*, 29 Jun. 1957). The one-page supplement was dominated by a justification of the agricultural arrangements of the E.E.C. and went a long way to try to reassure the doubts of the (for the S.F.I.O.) politically-important small producers. Ever since the 1890's, the agrarian programme of the party had essentially comprised a defence of small property (Hoffman, 1963, p. 409).

By 1957, however, the nature of the party's advocacy of the E.E.C. implied an acceptance of the reality of French economic recovery, and thus of both the ability and necessity for it to be exposed to foreign competition. This line of argument, common to the contributions of Jaquet, Le Bail and Pineau to the columns of *Le Populaire*, met with no challenge from within the party. Reservations, such as there were, came from estranged intellectuals such as the economist Charles Bettelheim, who saw these arguments as representative of the classic concepts of economic liberalism, with its emphasis upon the competitive benefits of market forces. Far from such competition entailing economic liberalism, Bettelheim saw it as the creator of monopoly capitalism and the ruination of 'tens of thousands of small enterprises' (*Fr.Ob.*, 21 Mar. 1957). It would lead to economic concentration in the already powerful industrial complex of the Ruhr and northern France, a process from which all France, and especially the still underdeveloped areas, would suffer. Bettelheim was expressing the classic defence of the traditional protective devices by which the weak and inefficient small producer had been protected for a hundred years.

83

Specifically 'socialist' reservations over acceptance of the Rome Treaties were entirely absent from any party debates at any level at this time. Indeed, opposition of any kind was wholly absent, it being left primarily to people like Mendès-France to warn of the alleged French inability to face German competition. All taint of anti-Germanism had disappeared: no one even defended the E.E.C. as a means of contributing to Franco-German reconciliation, for that, since the conclusion by the Mollet government of the Saar Agreements in October 1956, was no longer the issue it had been two years earlier, and it was left now to the P.C.F. to attack the 'Europe of the Six' as the Europe of 'clericals and reactionaries' (see Poulain, 1961).

Doctrinal introspection

Apart from the reasons already mentioned for Mollet's strong advocacy of the E.E.C. and Euratom Treaties, it is important to recall that in the late 1950's the party was in the process of what amounted to a debate on its doctrinal aims. Articles were appearing in such journals and periodicals as *La Revue Socialiste*, *France Observateur* and *L'Express*, written by Jules Moch, Gérard Jaquet, Paul Ramadier and others, and they generally involved a considerable retreat from any orthodoxy to which the party could still honestly lay claim. Paul Ramadier, writing in *La Socialisme Démocratique* in January 1958, advocated what for a French socialist was significant: an unreserved rejection of the Marxist prescription, holding that 'everyone is free to profess it in his heart of hearts, but adherence to it is no longer characteristic of the socialist of 1958'. Such frankness was revisionism indeed for the S.F.I.O. For Ramadier, the enemy was no longer capitalism, which had in any case been transformed from a system of private entrepreneurial ownership to one of planned technocracy. What stood now before Ramadier's socialist in his quest for individual fulfilment was the new technocratic leviathan; it was the traditional *cri de coeur* of French radicalism.

In 1962 a party policy statement emerged as the fruit of doctrinal introspection. The document affirmed the character, 'at the same time reformist and revolutionary', of French socialism. In the same terms it denounced the capitalist and Soviet systems, and called for political, economic and social democracy, disarmament, and the establishment of a federal republic uniting the European nations of the West with those of Africa wishing to cooperate with it. It was a traditionally ambivalent formula, in which left-wing terminology—talk of removing the 'heavy burdens on the working classes'—obscured a patent pragmatism. The S.F.I.O. produced no Bad Godesberg programme, but in spirit its leaders were there. An article by Gérard Jaquet in *Le Populaire* (29 March 1961) is illustrative of this point. Somewhat portentously entitled 'Socialism and the Construction of Europe', it demonstrated the real lack of substance in party theorizing. Socialism, he argued, having an international vocation, and by consequence, a European one also, had worked with all the militant Europeans in establishing the new community since the war. But their socialism required them to press for 'democratic planning responsive to the true needs of social justice and permitting the workers to play a decisive role'. For them to do so, and to clip the power of the technocrats both at European and national levels, a European parliament was necessary. Presumably, it was to be there, by application of their suffrage rights alone, that workers were to 'play a decisive role'.

For Jaquet the choice was a 'capitalist Europe' or a 'workers Europe', and he concluded that 'if the free world wishes to guard its liberty . . . a united Europe is necessary, because it offers a new structure', enabling it to take up the challenge posed by Soviet economic strength, a threat on which he dwelt long, and with some invective. Yet he was still anxious to emphasize what he saw to be the inability of capitalism to meet the Soviet threat, on account of its having reached its 'phase of decadence'. Nothing demonstrates better the French socialist's penchant for advocating the defence of a hypothetical workers-controlled, non-capitalist free world against the totalitarian Soviet autarchy of the east; such intermeshing of social-democratic and pre-1917 Marxist formulae was entirely typical of the S.F.I.O. But behind the confused invective and the ambiguous idealism lay the reality of the pre-occupation with combating Communism and the need for strong democratic institutions. The 'socialist' prescriptions of the S.F.I.O. for what, after all, was essentially to be a market-controlled fusion of the economies of six west-European states, were of no substance; indeed they barely existed.

Gaullism

The S.F.I.O. went into the Fifth Republic with a policy for European economic and political integration, based on support for supranational institutions, democratically controlled, and for Western defence based on the Atlantic Alliance. Gaullist policies, as they were to be revealed, posed a direct threat to both, and throughout the period of the Fifth Republic, the S.F.I.O. uncompromisingly denounced both the *Europe des patries* and *force de frappe* conceptions.

Both the major European parties, the M.R.P. and the S.F.I.O., began the Fifth Republic as members of De Gaulle's government. Mollet's decision to make the S.F.I.O. the 'avant garde' of the Fifth Republic caused renewed dissension in socialist ranks. It seems clear that the S.F.I.O.'s European commitment played some part in aligning the party with the Gaullists at least in the constitutional referendum in September 1958. Having contributed to the shaping of the new constitution, Mollet was in favour of socialists voting 'oui' in the referendum, but Defferre, wielding his bloc of Bouches-du-Rhône *mandats*, was opposed. Jean Monnet, however, realized that the accession to full power of De Gaulle would endanger the future of European integration unless men committed to the enterprise were behind him, and he was anxious that the *centriste* coalition being explored between Pineau, Jaquet and Gazier of the S.F.I.O. and Teitgen of the M.R.P., should materialize. In the event of it not doing so, however, he believed it essential that the S.F.I.O. should unitedly support the new régime for the sake of the European cause. These arguments, when put to Defferre, appeared to convince him and in return for concessions from Mollet over the party's Algerian policy, which Defferre thought illiberal, he agreed to Mollet's call for a united positive socialist vote in the referendum (*Fr.Ob.*, 28 Aug. 1948).

Socialist participation in the Gaullist régime did not, however, last long (until December 1958), and even the M.R.P. ministers (Pflimlin and four others) were moved to resign in May 1962 in protest against the anti-European orientation of Gaullist policies. These policies presented the S.F.I.O. with the opportunity to confirm, if confirmation were necessary, what had been for at least a decade its own international orientations, against which the Gaullist veto on British entry to the Common Market, the withdrawal of the French delegate from the Brussels negotiations in June 1965, the Franco-German treaty, the *force de frappe* and anti-Americanism all offended. *L'Europe des patries* was variously described as 'une monstruosité', 'une conception attardée' (*B.I.*, Apr./Jun. 1961). Gaullist policies

87

were seen as leading to the weakening of the whole Atlantic Alliance and the compromising of European economic expansion (*Le Pop.*, 13 May 1961). The party was able to pose the stark antithesis of the Gaullist national method with the socialist internationalist method. The socialist solution of a federal Europe with institutions able to limit sovereignty and to apply by democratic means a common policy, was counterposed to a Gaullist policy of fragile and temporary coalitions. 'We Socialists,' proclaimed Francis Vals, 'want a political Europe and it is clear that our conceptions are not shared by the Government. To a confederated Europe we prefer a federated Europe, to the Europe of *patries* we prefer the Europe of *peuples*' (*J.O.*, National Assembly, 16 Jun. 1961). The Gaullist proposal for a permanent Secretariat and regular head-of-state meetings was held to be in clear contradiction to the aim of building a political community based on democratic control through a directly-elected assembly: the Gaullist concept was autocratic; the socialist, democratic (Philip, *Le Pop.*, 4 Dec. 1961).

The Franco-German treaty was opposed because the reintegration of democratic Germany into the life of free peoples could only be achieved in the framework of a European community, which could nurture the young German democracy, and prevent a resurrection of nationalism. To believe that the question of Franco-German relations was of higher priority than European unification and could even be substituted for it, was to run the risk of reviving precisely those anti-democratic and nationalistic forces. The reversion of the French Government to traditional head-of-state diplomacy, which had never been successful in preventing war, threatened the internationalist goal of European supranationalism (Fuzier, Jan. 1963). The European community was in danger of finding itself seriously compromised and the Gaullist policy of false grandeur would inexorably lead to French isolation. Gaullist policies were tragically negative (Jaquet, *S.I.I.*, Jan. 1963).

In the sphere of defence, the *force de frappe* was denounced as threatening to the idea of integration, and against the spirit of Euratom, and NATO, which was 'the only defensive barrier for free Europe' (Mollet, *Le Pop.*, 25 Oct. 1960). The *force de frappe* was inspired by a 'detestable Americanophobia' and was condemned without reservation. The Stalinist tendency was still present in Russia and thus the maintenance of American forces in Europe was necessary as a symbol of essential free world solidarity (Pineau, *B.I.*, Apr. 1965).

All of this was easily said. It was fairly easy to be a true European in the face of Gaullist policies, in much the same way that it was easy during the 1964 American Presidential Election to be a liberal in the face of Senator Goldwater's pronouncements. A complete antithesis was possible, and whilst not questioning the essential sincerity of the S.F.I.O.'s Europeanism, there is little doubt that the European issue was used as a means of rallying against De Gaulle the various forces of the left, in a movement established in 1961, *La Gauche Européenne*. The movement, presided over by Gérard Jaquet, of the S.F.I.O.'s *Comité directeur*, was concerned with expounding the need for *l'Europe des travailleurs* as opposed to *l'Europe des patries*, which was possible only with the constitution of a supranational executive independent of governments and responsible to a directly-elected European parliament. To prevent the materialization of *l'Europe des patrons et patries* it was necessary to create *l'Europe de la planification démocratique*.

That the movement was not solely concerned, however, with the European question is revealed in speeches of delegates to its December 1961 Conference and by the motion

89

passed expressing 'recognition of the necessity of making contacts which would enable a regrouping of the forces of the Left' (*Le Pop.*, 4 Dec. 1961). A speech made by François Mitterrand (U.D.S.R.), pointing to the role *La Gauche Européenne* could play in helping the under-developed countries by fostering European integration and remarking that in this respect the policy of *La Gauche Européenne* was in sharp contrast to the policies of the French Government, indicated the way in which the issue was being used for domestic French political purposes. A motion concerning the French situation was passed by the Congress stating its wish to produce a regrouping of democrats of the left for the promotion of modern socialism, and to oppose any eventual fascist offensive (*Le Pop.*, 4 Dec. 1961).

That the 'European Idea' should be used as a means by which French leftwing forces engineered the creation of a coherent opposition to De Gaulle, does not detract from the S.F.I.O.'s long commitment to it. Indeed it could be seen in part as the very expression of the S.F.I.O.'s commitment to European integration : for this commitment was based essentially upon an unshaking belief in political democracy, a goal for which *La Gauche Européenne* was striving, both in the European community and in France.

8

Conclusion

That the S.F.I.O. has been by its official attitudes, and by substantial rank and file Congress majorities, a party favourable to European integration is confirmed. In fact, the party was second only to the M.R.P. in both commitment and in the extent to which it was able to maintain party unity on this issue. Until 1958 the S.F.I.O.'s National Assembly representation never fell below 95, and it was upon this substantial block of socialist deputies that every extension of European integration depended for support, as shown in 1954 when the party's division ensured the rejection of the European Defence Community. From 1947 to 1951 the party was an important element in the 'third force' coalition formed to combat the threat from the P.C.F. and the R.P.F. The coalition, consisting essentially of Socialists, Radicals and Christian Democrats, was incidentally a grouping of all the French parties favourable towards European integration and it was governments formed from this coalition that signed the Marshall Aid agreement, the Statute of the Council of Europe, the Atlantic Pact and the Treaty of Paris which established the Coal and Steel Community, and introduced the European Army plan.

The withdrawal of the socialists from this coalition in
1951 and their eventual replacement by a group of Social
Republicans (Gaullists), in itself representing the resurgence
in the 1951 elections of the political forces most hostile
to European integration (i.e. the Communists and the Gaullists) and which was symbolized by the removal of
Schuman from the Quai d'Orsay in 1953, had a profound
effect on French politics and not least on the furtherance
of the European idea, conditioning as it did to a considerable extent the collapse of the E.D.C. project. In 1956
the return to power of another centrist coalition, the Republican Front, and the formation of the Mollet Government in January of that year, undoubtedly contributed to
the *rélance européenne*, encouraging Europeans such as
Monnet and Spaak to capitalize on the existence of a
French Government favourable to the idea of European
integration, and to bring to fruition the plans for nuclear
and economic communities.

The role of socialist ideology

The major conclusion drawn from this study of the
S.F.I.O.'s attitude towards European integration is that both
the advocacy of integration by the party leadership and
consistently substantial majorities of congress, and the
hostility of the small anti-European minority, have been
characterized by the use of arguments entirely typical of
the political, rather than of the economic, left (a distinction defined in Chapter 1). This was not unquestionably
the case in the immediate post-war years when orthodox
Guesdist sentiment called for a United Socialist States of
Europe and a non-aligned international third force and
expressed its reservations of 'capitalistic' Marshall Aid,
but essentially such specifically socialist ideological arguments were characteristic of a pre-Cold War situation
92

when France was governed by an improbable coalition of communists, socialists and catholics, and when millenarial spirits were high in the party.

Such ideologically-inspired reasoning was to play no more than a minimal role in either the arguments of advocates or of opponents. There is no real evidence of the S.F.I.O. pursuing what could be interpreted as specifically socialist economic goals either in its domestic or foreign policies. In fact many economic questions at issue between parties in most democratic systems were not at issue in France. There had long been a wide consensus on the need for indicative planning and the Monnet plans instituted after the war did not meet any serious opposition—nor did Mendès-France's essentially 'New Deal' policies in 1954, or the technocratic planning of the Fifth Republic.

The existence of this consensus contributed to the decline of the S.F.I.O.'s interest in economic issues and economic planning, the advocacy of which did not distinguish it (Graham, pp. 50, 55). What did distinguish the S.F.I.O. was not its support for planning, but its insistence on popular control and participation in the planning (Caute, pp. 38, 43), and this it did both in the French and the European contexts, but even this should not be taken as implying very much. The Frankfurt Declaration of the Socialist International in 1952 stated that socialist planning 'does not presuppose public ownership of all the means of production', and there is no evidence of the S.F.I.O. delegates at Frankfurt dissenting from this view. The party had in reality succumbed to the seductions of the Keynesian or mixed economy, and was particularly anxious to reassure small producers of their respect for it. Hence Professor Weill-Reynal, writing in 1950, spoke of an 'economic order which respects the small entrepreneur in agriculture, industry and commerce' (*La Revue Social-*

iste, Jul. 1950). As with most policy statements on other issues, the S.F.I.O.'s economic policy declarations have normally been replete with orthodox-sounding rhetoric, accompanied by thoroughly equivocal word usage. As Micaud has pointed out: 'The S.F.I.O. is for raising wages, but not for the fiscal and social reforms that would permit a limitation on profits. It is for lowering the prices of vital necessities, but not for ending the subsidies to certain agricultural products. It is for economic expansion but not for dealing with marginal enterprises' (Micaud, 1963, p. 293). All these themes are common to most French parties, though the emphasis placed on one or other depends on the importance each party attaches to a particular following. In its support for economic radicalism, the S.F.I.O., claims Duverger, identifies itself more and more with French conservatism, the conservatism of the little people. By its parliamentary performance the party has done nothing to dispel an impression of a party in full sympathy with economic revisionism, and except in the early postwar years, there is no evidence of Europe being sponsored as a framework in which specifically socialist economic policies might be implemented, or of it being opposed on account of its being inspired by essentially liberal economic theories. Philip's defence of European integration in fact came very close to an argument *for* liberal economic policies and in so far as the party developed any clear position on an economic policy for European integration, it was based on the argument of the big market, promising as it allegedly did, immediate increased living standards for workers. The constantly reiterated demand for popular control of any European institutions set up is further evidence of the S.F.I.O.'s characteristic preoccupation with essentially liberal democratic values, a preoccupation which in fact implied revision of Bernstein's revisionism. Bernstein had written of the strategic implications of the

94

revisionist approach, arguing that liberal democracy could in fact be a prelude to socialist democracy. The S.F.I.O. in its European policy seemed to confirm its complete acceptance of the former, with all the short-term electoral hopes it seemed to sustain, whilst relegating the latter to the status of rhetorical orations at annual congresses.

If the S.F.I.O. nurtured any economic reservations on European integration, they were not of a socialist character, but were, as Philip has indicated, the reservations of the small producer, hankering after protection from vastly superior foreign competitors. The 'Radicalization' of the party from the 1930's onwards, and the entering into its ranks of many such petit-bourgeois elements in the industrially inefficient south and west of France, undoubtedly determined that the party's reservations to economic integration would be conditioned by an essentially 'Radical' resentment of foreign economic efficiency.

If one thus reduces the strictly ideological motivation of the S.F.I.O.'s European policy to no more than a minor role, the real nature of its motivation remains to be defined. Essentially political and basically negative, the mainsprings of the party's pro-Europeanism seem to have lain in its *anti-Communism and anti-Germanism*.

Anti-Communism

The S.F.I.O. had a long history of almost obsessive anti-Communism long before the Cold War gave it a general impetus in the late 1940's. The original S.F.I.O., established in 1905 and, under Jaurès's influence, given over to the reformist cause, had witnessed at the Tours Congress of 1920 a revolt of over three quarters of the membership, who voted to rename the party, *Parti communiste français*. The reformist minority rump retained the name S.F.I.O. Thus it was that the formation of the French Communist

Party had been the result of an internecine revolt in the S.F.I.O. and not only had a rival working-class party been created, but its creation was a result of the S.F.I.O. being, in effect, occupied by the bolsheviks, leaving a tremendous psychological scar on the emasculated, reformist rump. In addition, the P.C.F. grew numerically into the second largest Communist party in Western Europe, emerging in 1946 as the strongest party in France with nearly 29% of the votes, and, by its conquest in the late 1940's of the C.G.T., the manipulator of an organization representing the great majority of the French working class.

The S.F.I.O. is a party whose working-class vote by 1951 comprised but one fifth of its total and of whose party candidates only 7% were working class, whilst over a third of its party representatives were schoolteachers and most of its popular support consisted of middle-class *fonctionnaires* and teachers (Duverger, *Les Temps Modernes*, 1955). To such a party, ostensibly of Marx and for revolution, the existence of the P.C.F. has always stood as a humiliating reminder of its impotence. The party has long struggled to regain the loyalties of the French working class but without success. The persistently monolithic presence of the P.C.F. stood testimony to this failure. To compensate for its humiliation, the S.F.I.O. has been at pains to assert its claim to be the only true party of the left; the only party faithful to the real interests of the proletariat. The P.C.F. was not of the left, it claimed, but of the East. It was no more than the vehicle for Stalinist aggression. It was the alien, Russian party, which had concluded the pact with Nazi Germany in 1939.

Allied to and reflected in its anti-Communism was the S.F.I.O.'s ardent commitment to the defence of political democracy and the parliamentary republic. This characteristic served both to distinguish it from the P.C.F. and to draw it into coalitions of Republican defence, for ex-

96

ample in 1947 and, if Mollet is to be believed, in 1958. The fact that the socialists were in partnership with conservative parties in the third force coalition (which was directed ostensibly against the dual threat from the P.C.F. and the R.P.F.) and that they were tied by their commitment to defend the régime, and this in the context of the Cold War, led the party increasingly into anti-Communist attitudes. Its involvement in the defence of liberal democratic political values could not but involve it in the defence of non-Communist Europe from what it saw to be the threat of Soviet aggression.

The S.F.I.O. was thus able to arrive at an intellectual justification of NATO by virtue of its concern with purely political issues. It is true that attempts were made to erect a third force superstructure upon the obviously Atlanticist and American-dominated basis of NATO, in order to accommodate certain ideological objections to the Atlantic Pact, from a handful of pacifists and neutralists who believed in the possibility of peaceful co-existence with the East. In fact, of course, Mollet's advocacy of 'a Europe not neutral but independent', playing a role between the U.S.A. and U.S.S.R., was a meaningless form of words, an attempted rationalization of an impracticable conception which was crushed in the light of the necessity of making a choice between the two real alternatives. Apart from the third force concept—strong in the pre-Cold War period but progressively forgotten in the 1950's—the S.F.I.O.'s advocacy of Western defence has come the closest of any of its policy statements to being unequivocal. Mollet has spoken of the party being 'on the side of the West and intending to remain there', and of NATO being 'Europe's shield . . . which has ensured the maintenance of liberty' (Mollet, 1958). The S.F.I.O.'s unambiguous defence of the Atlantic Pact rests essentially upon its deep-seated hostility and defensive reaction to Communism.

Anti-Germanism

If the party's commitment to western defence, as represented by NATO and W.E.U., was basically conditioned by
its anti-Communism, its acceptance of all aspects of European integration rested as much upon its anti-Germanism,
though this was a more complex factor, for it was one
which the opposing forces within the party both used in
pursuit of their differing goals.

The leadership clearly saw European integration as a
means of providing a context for a controlled German
revival, functional institutions like the Coal and Steel Community and the European Defence Community being con-
ducive to this end. Seen at its best, the party's policy was
formed in the spirit of Blum's advocacy in *A L'échelle
humaine* of the creation of a European order in which
German reconstruction after wartime defeat could be
accomplished, a democratic order in which a new German
democracy could be established on equal status with the
other countries of Europe. Seen in a more negative light,
and by the majority of the party militants, the policy,
for example in the case of the Coal and Steel Community,
provided the means of preventing the re-establishing of an
arsenal on the Ruhr, and thus of avoiding the fourth war
of German aggression since 1870. The motive was repressive.

In 1954, at the height of the E.D.C. controversy, an example was provided of the dual use of anti-Germanism
in the party, the leadership posing E.D.C. as a means of
containing the alleged German menace, and the opposition
group depicting E.D.C. as a vehicle for a resurrection of
the Wehrmacht and thus of renewed German aggression.
Advocacy or hostility to European integration, as represented by E.D.C., was determined by the relative degree
of emphasis which the party militant placed upon his anti-

Communism or his anti-Germanism. To Mollet it was the bolshevik threat that was paramount; to Mayer it was the possible resurgence of a Nazi Germany. In neither case can purely ideological considerations be said to have played much part: Mayer, for example, though joined in his opposition by some who disliked the anti-Communist bias of Mollet's argument, was motivated essentially by an emotional antipathy towards Germany.

In fact, the basically non-ideological nature of the arguments which the party advanced for European integration was also characteristic of the arguments of those hostile to integration. Socialist ideological preoccupations did, it has been admitted, condition the neutralism of the third force advocates and the anti-capitalism of those opposed to economic integration, but essentially the opposition was motivated by factors utterly foreign to the socialist canon as understood in most Western European countries.

The opposition was motivated primarily by an almost xenophobic distrust of Germany, and a fear that the Europe being integrated would be clerical and reactionary. On all counts a case could thus be made for the British presence, but the reiterated demand for this presence cloaked with an apparent rationality what was essentially an emotional case. The nature of the opposition, based upon the old radical causes of *laïcité* and popular sovereignty, reflected the extent to which factors characteristic of the political, rather than the economic, left, were conditioning S.F.I.O. attitudes to European integration. The expressions of hostility between 1952 and 1954 towards the clerical and reactionary nature of the 'Europe of the Six' reflected the militants' conception of Jacobin democracy, dating from the heroic period at the turn of the century when socialist activists took up the defence of democracy, seeing themselves as self-appointed champions of reason, progress and justice, and as the vanguard

99

of the republican army of liberation. Most of the prominent socialists (*viz* Lacoste, Moch, Naegelen, and Lejeune)
who rebelled over the E.D.C. issue in 1954 represented
precisely this strain of radical, Jacobin patriotism. All
resolutely on the right of the party, their's was not a protest against a 'capitalist' Europe (*Fr.Ob.*, 3 Feb. 1955).
André Philip was right to draw attention to the fact that
hostility to the little Europe of the Six, as represented in
the E.D.C. plan, was centred in the west, south-west and
Midi, whose economic backwardness (and therefore vul-
nerability to German competition) was but one manifesta-
tion of a strongly-entrenched traditionalist ethos frequently
expressing itself in radical outbursts of republicanism, anti-
clericalism, and *anti-dirigisme*. The influence of this France
on the S.F.I.O. had grown immeasurably in the inter- and
post-war years. Political individualism, and a political
psychology more adapted to resistance than to positive
construction, a product of an atomized, small-scale, small-
enterprise society, had come to dominate the S.F.I.O.

The role of the S.F.I.O.'s internationalist theory remains
to be assessed. The humanitarian universalism of Jean
Jaurès and Léon Blum, presenting as it did further confirmation of the S.F.I.O.'s revisionist stance and radicalized
outlook, clearly provided the intellectual backcloth of the
party's European policy. Without it the policy would have
lacked coherence. Yet it is impossible to claim for the
party's internationalism a significant role in the evolution
of its European policy, which was fashioned basically by
the need to contain German resurgence and provide a defence of Western Europe. Nonetheless, the party had remained true to socialist internationalism, as Blum had
interpreted it, despite the necessity of accepting the progressive limitation of its scope to the Communities of the
Six, a restriction from which the party has genuinely de-
sired to break free and to secure the adhesion to the Com-

munity treaties of as many member states as possible, particularly the north European social democracies.

It would, however, be foolish to credit the official party dispositions with too much altruistic content. The S.F.I.O.'s preoccupations were essentially with its electoral position in France and its foreign policy was bound to be sub-ordinated to the requirements of domestic politics as it saw them. As has been shown, the party was not averse to using the European issue as a means of forging coalitions which could return it to power.

Escapist illusion

It has been argued that the S.F.I.O.'s Europeanism has been the product of a complete escapism. Speaking primarily of the E.D.C., but with the whole process of European integration in mind, Duverger argued that the construction of Europe constituted 'a false problem, an alibi for refusing to face the real question. For the Socialists, as for the Catholic *cédistes*, the myth of a supranational Europe was a means of escaping an unbearable reality by finding a refuge in an imaginary world: by multiplying by six all the contradictions and the helplessness in which we find ourselves, they could have been miraculously resolved' (Duverger, 1955). The accusation of escapism is somewhat unfair in that it could also be applied with possibly greater force to the opponents of integration who were declining to accept the reality of interdependence, believing that France's problems could be resolved through isolation.

There is, however, some evidence to suggest that the S.F.I.O. leadership, after years of anxious and hopeless mauoeuvrings for power in France, a process which had led to the erosion of its doctrine and programme, and their sacrifice upon the altar of political opportunism, was look-ing towards Europe as a context in which the party could regain some of its self-respect. The new Europe would be anti-Communist: Communists could be excluded from all key posts and could be deprived of all prospects of a seizure of power, and possibly also of their grip over the French and Italian working-class movements. Not only would a united Europe mean fast economic expansion and higher living standards, but also the likelihood that the strong socialist contingents from Germany and the Low Countries would, with or without British participation, greatly strengthen socialism, and weaken Communism in France and Italy. Mollet himself suggested that such reasoning was his: 'We know that events would rapidly sweep Europe along the road to Socialism' (Werth, 1956, p. 432). No longer would the party be outflanked by the Communists or forced to support one form of anti-socialism against another, as the Fourth Republic system dictated, but instead socialism could appear as the wave of the future, harnessing the theme of the New Europe to its advantage.

Jaquet enlarged on this theme in March 1961 when he emphasized the need for the 'solidarity of all democratic forces of the left' including the unions in the European community, and talked of understanding 'the importance of the European mission which we take up' (Jaquet, *Le Pop.*, 29 Mar. 1961).

As regards the party militants, there is considerable evidence that their reaction to the European question involved a strong element of escapism, disinclined to come to terms with new problems and unthinkingly loyal as they were to a host of doctrinal shibboleths, such as the anti-clerical issue, with which the contemporary world was not concerned, and for the accommodation of which no provision was therefore made. Undoubtedly the rebellion over the E.D.C. question, in which all the conditioned reflexes of the militants were indulged, had an unmistakably cathartic character, as if the rank and file were rebelling not so much against their leaders (though Mollet's dictatorial technique was at issue) or even against European integration *per se*, but against their situation and the intolerable frustrations placed upon them by the party's involvement in at first tripartite and later centrist coalitions which unfailingly involved the total submergence of the S.F.I.O.'s political identity. In these senses, therefore, the allegation of escapism is valid.

By the nature of its advocacy of European integration, the French Socialist Party has demonstrated its essential characteristics of reformism and radicalism, and shown itself to be a party wholly of the political left. Guesde, whose socialism had its origins in the economic phenomena which he and his orthodox contemporaries identified with capitalism, and who saw the issues of 'école laïque' and republican defence as mere diversions from the main economic aims of socialism, had denounced Jaurèsian socialism as the prolongation of the consummation of the democratic movement which issued from the 'bourgeois' revolution at the end of the eighteenth century. In its advocacy of European integration the party has shown that this analysis of Jaurèsian socialism is equally applicable to the modern party's European policy. In the words of Christian Pineau (*S.I.I.*, Jan. 1967): 'Socialists are enthusiastic supporters of the unification of Europe as a prelude to the unification of the planet, but they are realists, and are aware of the difficulties and of the time which this will take. Above all, they do not intend to sacrifice to the future the political democracy which forms the basis of their beliefs. The expression "free world" still has a meaning for them; for them the future is not Aldous Huxley's best of possible worlds, but a world in which man remains an individual, in which co-operation is an accepted practice and in which the freedom of the people is preserved.'

Appendix: Chronological summary of European organizations

April 1948   O.E.E.C.: an intergovernmental organization, set up to distribute Marshall Aid, co-ordinate investment programmes and revive inter-European trade; 16 member states.

May 1949   Council of Europe set up as a result of a call for economic and political integration and a parliamentary assembly for Western Europe, made at the Hague Congress of European federalists in May 1948. Two main political organs:
(i) Committee of Ministers (usually composed of member-state foreign ministers). Major decisions require majority vote.
(ii) Consultative Assembly (representatives sent from the member-state parliaments). No legislative power; no executive responsible to it. Valuable as a forum for European propagandists, who used it to demand creation of a European supranational authority with real powers, i.e. involving the diminution of national sovereignty, which Britain and Scandinavian states opposed.

May 1950   Schuman Plan: intended as the first step to-
            wards a European federation, with Franco-
            German reconciliation as its kernel.

April 1951 E.C.S.C.: the entire coal and steel produc-
            tion of France, West Germany, Italy and the
            Benelux countries placed under a common
            High Authority. The first organization of the
            'Six', and the first of the functionalist type.
            Preamble to the E.C.S.C. treaty committed
            the Six to a full European economic com-
            munity at some future date.
            Institutions:
              High Authority: 9 independent members;
              represents the supranational, or com-
              munity, interest.
              Council of Ministers: representatives
              (normally foreign ministers) of the mem-
              ber states.
              Common Assembly and *Court of Justice*.
            This basic institutional plan formed the blue-
            print for the future.

April 1951 E.D.C. proposed. A European Army to be
            set up, to which all member states would
            contribute, including West Germany. To be
            under a joint European control, with institu-
            tions of the same type as in the E.C.S.C., ex-
            cept that there would be provision for a
            directly elected Assembly. Proposal rejected
            by France in August 1954.

December   W.E.U. An alternative to E.D.C. Britain and
1954   the Six to control German rearmament. West
            Germany to be made a sovereign state and
            admitted to NATO.

July 1955   Messina Conference opened to consider establishing economic and atomic energy communities on the E.C.S.C. pattern. Discussions in an intergovernmental committee of experts from the Six led to the Rome Treaties of March 1957.

March 1957   Establishment of E.E.C. and Euratom. E.E.C. treaty set out a plan for the creation of a common market over a 12-year period, the evolution of a single market being seen as a step towards eventual political integration.

Suggestions for further reading

Literature on the French Socialist Party and on the question of socialist parties' attitudes towards European integration is not extensive.

Incomparably the best book in English on French politics in general, for the period covered by this book, and which includes a useful chapter on the S.F.I.O., is Philip Williams' *Crisis and Compromise* (Longmans, 1964). D. Ligou's *Histoire du Socialisme en France* (Presses Universitaires de France, 1962) and André Philip's *Les Socialistes* (Éditions du Seuil, 1967), are two of the better histories of the party; Philip's book covers aspects of the European policy well, though suffers in part for being somewhat polemical. C. A. Micaud's *Communism and the French Left* (New York, 1963) provides a very good study of the S.F.I.O. within the general context of the left.

The French Socialists and Tripartisme, 1944-1947, by B. D. Graham (Weidenfeld, 1965) is a helpful study of the S.F.I.O. in the immediate post-war years, and contains a summary of the doctrinal argument in the party in the mid-1940's, and is a good sequel to the study of doctrinal dispute contained in A. Noland's *The Founding of the French Socialist Party* (Harvard, 1958). On revisionist socialist parties in general, Peter Gay's *The Dilemma of Democratic Socialism* (Columbia, 1952) contains an excellent examination of the ideological basis of social democratic parties, and of their tactical problems.

France: Change and Tradition, by S. Hoffman (Gollancz, 1963), is a good background work, examining as it does the important processes of transformation at work in French society, and includes a chapter on French foreign policy since 1945, though for a much fuller account of this, A. Grosser's *La politique extérieure de la IVe République* (Éditions du Seuil, 1965) should be used.

E. B. Haas's *The Uniting of Europe* (1958) and A. Zurcher's *The Struggle to Unite Europe* (1958), cover the process of European integration since the war. Haas concentrates on the institutional aspects, and includes a short section on the attitudes taken up by the French parliament and parties, whilst Zurcher's approach is more historical, and provides a good chronological account. The aspect of integration which has received more coverage than any other is the collapse of the E.D.C. project in August 1954, and the best study of this may be found in *France Defeats E.D.C.*, by D. Lerner and R. Aron (Praeger, 1957). F. Roy Willis's *France, Germany and the New Europe* (Stanford, 1965) provides a detailed study of the integration process as it affected France and West Germany from the end of the war to the early 1960's.

Bibliography

ARON, R. (1960) *France Steadfast and Changing*, Harvard.

BARRON, R. (1959) *Parties and Politics in Modern France*, Public Affairs Press.

BERNSTEIN, E. (1961) *Evolutionary Socialism* (1909), Schocken.

BETTELHEIM, C. 'Le Marché Commun', *France Observateur*, 21 March 1957.

BLUM, LÉON (1946) *A l'Échelle Humaine* (Trans. by W. Pickles), Gollancz.

BLUM, LÉON 'Notes sur la doctrine', *La Revue Socialiste*, July 1946.

BOURDET, C. 'Les Élections dans l'Europe Vaticane', *France Observateur*, 27 May 1954.

BOURGIN, G. 'Vers la Fédération européenne,' *La Revue Socialiste*, January 1951.

CAUTE, D. (1966) *The Left in Europe*, World University Library.

CODDING, G. 'The French Socialist Party and the West', *Orbis*, Winter 1961.

COLTON, J. 'Léon Blum and the French Socialists as a Government Party', *The Journal of Politics*, Gainesville, XV, no. 4, November 1953.

COMMIN, P. *Socialist International Information*, 6 January 1951.

COURTIEU, P. 'Le projet de programme fondamental du parti socialiste S.F.I.O.', *Cahiers du Communisme*, April 1961.

DIEBOLD, W. (1959) *The Schuman Plan*, Praeger.

DUVERGER, M. (1954) *Political Parties*, Methuen.

DUVERGER, M. 'S.F.I.O.: Mort ou Transfiguration', *Les Temps Modernes*, nos. 112-113, 1955.

ENSOR, R. C. K. (1908) *Modern Socialism*, Harper.

ESTIER, C. 'Le "59" veulent sauver l'unité de la S.F.I.O.', *L'Observateur d'aujourd'hui*, 8 April 1954.

ESTIER, C. 'Guy Mollet n'a pas vaincu l'opposition socialiste à la C.E.D.', *France Observateur*, 3 June 1954.

ESTIER, C. 'La "petite Europe" revient en scène', *France Observateur*, 27 December 1956.

FAUVET, J. (1957) *France Defeats E.D.C.* (ed. Lerner and Aron), Praeger.

FAUVET, J. (1959) *La IVe République*, A. Fayard.

FREYMOND, J. (1964) *Western Europe since the War*, Pall Mall.

FREYMOND, J. (1960) *The Saar Conflict*, Stevens.

FRIED, A. and SANDERS, R. (1964) *Socialist Thought: A Documentary History*, Edinburgh University Press.

FUZIER, C. 'Le traité Franco-Allemand et l'Europe', *Democratie 63*, Paris, January 1963.

GAY, P. (1952) *The Dilemma of Democratic Socialism*, Columbia University Press.

GERBET, P. 'La France et l'organisation de l'Europe', *Tendances*, September 1960.

GOGUEL, F. (1952) *France under the Fourth Republic*, Cornell University Press.

GRAHAM, B. D. (1965) *The French Socialists and Tripartisme, 1944-1947*, Weidenfeld.

GRAY, A. (1963 edn.) *The Socialist Tradition*, Longmans.

GROSSER, A. (1961) *La politique extérieure de la IVe République*, Éditions du Seuil.

GUESDE, J. (and JAURÈS, J.) (1945) *Les Deux Méthodes*, Paris.

GUESDE, J. (1944) *Le Socialisme*, Paris.

HAAS, E. B. (1958) *The Uniting of Europe*, Stevens.

HALLSTEIN, W. (1962) *United Europe*, Oxford University Press.

HALPERIN, S. W. (1946) 'Léon Blum and Contemporary French Socialism', *The Journal of Modern History*, Chicago, xviii, September 1946.

HOFFMAN, S. (1963) *France: Change and Tradition*, Gollancz.

HURTIG, S. 'La S.F.I.O. face à la Ve République', *Revue française de science politique*, June 1964.

JAQUET, G. 'La prochaine étape', *Le Populaire*, 1 January, 1955.

JAQUET, G. 'Le socialisme et la construction européenne', *Le Populaire*, 29 March 1961.

JAQUET, G. 'De Gaulle and Great Britain', *Socialist International Information*, January 1963.

JAURÈS, J. (1895) *Idealism in History*.

JAURÈS, J. (1906) *Studies in Socialism*.

LAPIE, P.-O. (1960) *Les Trois Communautés*, A. Fayard.

LIGOU, D. (1962) *Histoire du Socialisme en France 1871-1961*, Presses Universitaires de France.

LERNER, D. and ARON, R. (1957) *France Defeats E.D.C.*, Praeger.

LOCKWOOD, T. G. 'A Study of French Socialist Ideology', *Review of Politics*, xxi, April 1959.

LORWIN, V. R. (1954) *The French Labor Movement*, Harvard.

LUETHY, H. (1955) *France Against Herself*, Praeger.

MACRIDIS, R. C. 'The Predicament of French Socialism', *Antioch Review*, Autumn 1960.

MARCUS, J. T. (1958) *Neutralism and Nationalism in France*, Bookman.

MAYNE, R. (1964) *The Community of Europe*, Gollancz.

MICAUD, C. (1956) 'French Political Parties: Ideological Myths and Social Realities', in *Modern Political Parties: Approaches to Comparative Politics*, S. Neumann (ed.), Chicago.

MICAUD, C. A. (1963) *Communism and the French Left*, New York.

MICHELS, R. (1962 edn.) *Political Parties*, Collier Books.

MOCH, J. 'L'heure du socialisme', *B.I. du parti socialiste S.F.I.O.*, January 1945.

MOCH, J. 'Rethinking Socialism', *La Revue Socialiste*, April 1959.

MOLLET, G. (1951) *L'Action socialiste au cours de la Législature 1946-51: pour la défense de la République, de la Liberté et de la Paix*, Arras.

MOLLET, G. 'A Warning', *Europe Today and Tomorrow*, December 1952.

MOLLET, G. 'Socialists and the European Army', *Socialist International Information*, 2 February 1952.

MOLLET, G. 'The European Problem', *Socialist International Information*, 29 November 1952.

MOLLET, G. 'France and the Defence of Europe', *Foreign Affairs*, April 1954.

MOLLET, G. 'L'Unification de l'Europe', *Monde Nouveau Paru*, November 1955.

MOLLET, G. (1958) *Bilan et perspectives socialistes*, Paris, pp. 8-21.

MOLLET, G. *La Documentation socialistes*, No. 4, April 1958, p. 3.

NOLAND, A. (1956) *The Founding of the French Socialist Party 1895-1905*, Harvard.

PHILIP, A. (1951) *The Schuman Plan—Nucleus of a European Community*.

PHILIP, A. (1951) *L'Unité européenne—L'heure de décision*.

PHILIP, A. (1953) *L'Europe unie et sa place dans l'Économie internationale*, Presse Universitaire de France.

PHILIP, A. (1957) *France Defeats E.D.C.*, Praeger.

PHILIP, A. (1957) *Le Socialisme Trahi*, Plon.

PHILIP, A. 'Europe des affaires ou Europe démocratique', *Le Populaire*, 4 December 1961.

PHILIP, A. (1967) *Les Socialistes*, Éditions du Seuil.

PICKLES, D. (1955) *France, the Fourth Republic*, Methuen.

PICKLES, D. (1960) *The Fifth French Republic*, Methuen.

PINEAU, C. 'The Problem of Gaullism', *Socialist International Information*, 21 January 1967.

PIVERT, M. 'USA-Europe-USSR: la position socialiste', *La Revue Socialiste*, December 1947.

Political and Economic Planning Report, 'France and the European Community', 1961.

POULAN, J. C. 'Le Parti S.F.I.O. et l'Intégration européenne', *Cahiers du Communisme*, April 1961.

RACIER, R. 'Quatre tendances au sein du parti socialiste', *France Observateur*, 3 February 1955.

RAMADIER, P. 'Socialist ideas, theory and practice', *Le Socialisme Démocratique*, Geneva, January-March 1958.

RAYNAL, W. 'The French Socialist Party—its role', *La Revue Socialiste*, July 1950 (Reprinted in *S.I.I.*, August 1950).

RIMBERT, P. 'L'Avenir du parti socialiste', *La Revue Socialiste*, February 1952.

RIMBERT, P. (1955) 'Le Parti Socialiste S.F.I.O.', in *Partis politiques et classes sociales en France*, ed. M. Duverger.

RUBEL, M. 'Léon Blum et la doctrine socialiste', *La Revue Socialiste*, nos. 38-9, 1949.

SIMMONS, H. G. 'The French Socialist Party, 1956-66', unpublished Ph.D. thesis, Cornell University, 1967.

S.F.I.O. 'Programme fondamental du parti socialiste', *La Revue Socialiste*, July 1959.

VERDIER, R, (1945) *École Laïque et Liberté*.

VOYENNE, B. (1954) *Petite Histoire de l'Idée Européenne*, Peyot.

WEINSTEIN, H, (1936) *Jeau Jaurès: A Study of Patriotism in the French Socialist Movement*, Columbia University Press.

WERTH, A. (1956) *France 1940-55*, Hale.

WILLIAMS, P. (1954) *Politics in Post-War France*, Longmans.

WILLIAMS, P. (1964) *Crisis and Compromise*, Longmans.

WILLIS, R. (1965) *France, Germany and the New Europe*, Stanford University Press.

ZWICHER, A. (1958) *The Struggle to Unite Europe*, New York Oxford University Press.